The New Generation Gap

MICHELLE DAGNINO WITH CAROLINE FERNANDEZ

The New Generation Gap

Order this book online at www.trafford.com
or email orders@trafford.com

Most Trafford titles are also available at major online book retailers.

info@michelledagnino.com • www.michelledagnino.com

Printed in the United States of America.

ISBN: 978-1-4269-7056-6 (sc)

Trafford rev. 10/06/2011

   www.trafford.com

North America & International
toll-free: 1 888 232 4444 (USA & Canada)
phone: 250 383 6864 ♦ fax: 812 355 4082

CONTENTS

PREFACE

Why does this topic – understanding and engaging with the four generations in the workplace – matter? Why should organizations care about the generational differences amongst their workforce?

My father once told me a story that highlighted the importance of this issue, and the impact that generational differences can have in our relationships and interactions with our colleagues, families and friends. Here is the story told by my father:

> It was a brisk night in early December, and I was alone in the house. Your mom had gone out with some friends and I was unpacking. You see, we had just moved into the house a week earlier, and we had a house filled with boxes. We hadn't had a chance to meet any of the neighbors yet, and we still were getting to know the neighborhood. I had the radio on in the background, but wasn't listening very closely to the program that was on. All of a sudden, an announcer broke into the program and it caught my attention. First, because it was past midnight, an unusual time for breaking news. Second, the tone of the announcer's voice gave me pause. He sounded…saddened. As I walked over to the radio to turn the volume up, I heard the announcer say, "It is with great sadness that I report that John Lennon was announced dead earlier today after being shot outside his place of residence in New York City." My heart skipped a beat when I heard his words, and I turned up the volume as high as it could go. After a few

more minutes, I realized it was true. We hadn't had the cable installed and I was anxious for more information. I stepped outside our front door, thinking perhaps I could walk to a late night pub. Yet when I stepped outside, I saw a group of neighbors gathered in the street. As I grabbed my coat to walk outside, they all turned to me, with the same sadness on their faces that I was feeling. Somebody said to me: "Heard the news?" I nodded my head in agreement and joined the group. For the rest of the evening, and well into the wee hours of the morning, we gathered, going from one house to another, watching television reports, playing Beatles and Lennon records, and exchanging stories about our first encounters with the music of John Lennon.

When I asked my father was this had to do with the work I was doing about managing different generations in the workplace he responded:

That moment in December 1981 was a life-changing moment that I shared with perfect strangers, dozens of people who I never met before, who were all brought together through this news. As my daughter, this is yet just another story your old dad is going on about. But for all of us who gathered together that night, we were brought together by a common experience. Regardless of our backgrounds, John Lennon was a common thread we shared with others of our generation. All the people that gathered in the street that night were of the same generation – Baby Boomers who realized that the death of John Lennon signified so much more than the loss of a great musician, but also provoked memories of first loves, broken hearts, struggles at homes, struggles on the street – for peace, for equal rights. These common moments were all shared by strangers because we were all members of the same generation.

Understanding how the generations interact with each other and the values that have shaped the lens through which they view the world is crucial information for anyone seeking to build an understanding of how to create a culture of innovation, creativity and supportive collaboration in the workplace. The experiences that we were raised with have influenced how we approach our work, our families and our communities. The pivotal moments in history shared across cultures and regions, means that we often have more shared experiences with our generational peers than we do with our children. Understanding that these experiences have informed the values that we bring to the workplace, will help us all navigate managing and leading across the generations more effectively.

For the first time since homesteading families laboured side-by-side building their future together, four generations of workers are now again working side by side, yet in a very different work environment. Significant changes to the workplace, from the introduction of just in time production to the influence of Generation Y, who are shaking up traditional workplace structures, we now have four generations, representing an age gap of up to 50 years between the youngest and the oldest, working together.

Yet, the four generations currently in the workplace - the Silent Generation, Baby Boomers, Generation X and Generation Y are not always working in harmony. Misunderstandings and conflict between the generations, impeding production and affecting performance is leading to a **New Generation Gap**.

To demystify the new generation gap one must understand the generations and generational divides. By understanding the general history, influence, experiences and values of a generation one can begin to comprehend what drives individual motivation, desire and goals.

For the purposes of this book, there are generalizations – as well as exceptions to generalizations concerning the four generations in the current workforce. These generations are supported by hypothesis.

Evidence indicates that we can rightly infer directional trends with the four working generations.

For the purposes of this book, identities have been given to the respective generations for the creative examples:

Silent Generation Sam   Baby Boomer Barb
Generation X Xavier   Generation Y Yasmin

The Silent Generation, Baby Boomers, Generation X and Generation Y are four generations who possess complimentary skills and tools for potentially great performance.

The premise of this book is to lay bare the generations, expose the nature of the New Generation Gap, bridge conflict and harness the power of four working generations to create an innovative team.

> *"People resemble their times more than they resemble their parents"*
> *-- Old Adage*

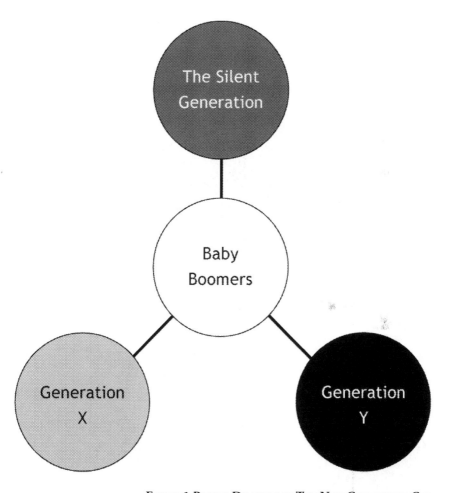

FIGURE 1 RADIAL DIAGRAM OF THE NEW GENERATION GAP

Chapter

1

UNDERSTANDING THE GENERATIONS

> *"Each generation imagines itself to be more intelligent than the one that went before it, and wiser than the one that comes after it."*
> **--George Orwell**

To fully understand the New Generation Gap, one must understand each generation according to their own contemporary and historically situated experiences. Historic events, generational norms, societal trends and pop culture are some of the factors contributing to the core values of a generation. Each generation's specific experience influences the attitudes that they bring into the modern office environment and the lens through which they view the world.

Let us start our investigation into bridging the new generation gap by investigating the history, culture and influencers of each specific generation.

Dark Grey – Managers
Light Grey – Mid-level management
Black – Front line staff
White - Other

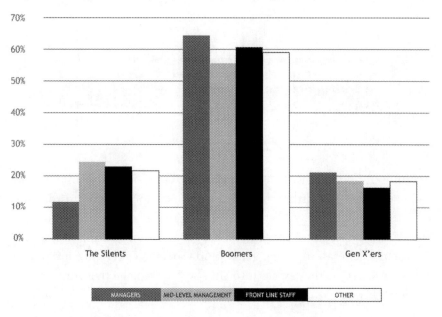

FIGURE 2 BREAKDOWN OF JOB ROLES IN THE MULTI-GENERATIONAL WORKPLACE

The Silent Generation

Born: 1922-1945
[Also known as: Silents, Seniors, Old Boys' Club,
Veterans, Veteran Generation, Mature Generation]

The Silent Generation was born into the tough economic times of the Great Depression and its subsequent years. The Great Depression was spurned on by "Black Thursday", October 24, 1929 - the date of the infamous United States stock market crash. As a result, commerce failed, unemployment numbers rose and financial resources dissipated. Industries and individuals suffered. Life was hard and bleak.

It was a time where children abandoned education to go to work (if any could be found) to help the family. These children of the Depression witnessed the frustration and suffering experienced by their parents. The innocence usually associated with childhood was short-lived in the lives of the Silent Generation.

> ### 30s Play list
>
> **Gorney and Harburg's** *"Brother, Can You Spare a Dime?"*
>
> **Irving Berlin's** *"Across The Breakfast Table (Looking At You)"*
>
> **Gershwin's** *"Embraceable You"*

On the heels of the Great Depression came the Second World War (1939-1945). Sons and daughters saw their fathers, uncles and brothers go to war. Ration coupons (for coffee, tea, sugar, and other food staples) were a mainstay to help families survive the war efforts.

The Silent Generation came of age seeing the return of wounded veterans, reading notifications of soldiers missing in action and grieving the loss of men who would not come back at all.

The Silent Generation's formative years were filled with sacrifice, hard work and suffering. They lived day-to-day as the future was too uncertain for plans. Their custom was - and still is - to make do with little resources. To waste not, want not.

Post-war, the Silent Generation entered into a very formal and hierarchical workforce. With little education, most new hires started in jobs on the factory floors and worked their way up through hard work, dedication and loyalty. There was a clear separation of gender and race in the work environment.

40's Play list

Jazz great Louis Armstrong forms his All Star Jazz ensemble

Edwards' *"When you wish upon a star"*

Davis' *"You are my Sunshine"*

The Silent Generation interacted with only same-level-employees and their direct supervisors. It was a male dominated work environment where relationships had strict boundaries (i.e. employees would use the courtesy title of "Mr." when speaking with superiors).

There was also clear work/life separation - men went to out to the paid workforce while women stayed at home to raise the children and tend to their houses.

Summation: The Silent Generation is a proven hard-working, loyal generation. They were the founders and leaders of many of today's most trusted corporate names. They valued hard work and street smarts as the path to success. Though they may not have much formal education accreditation, they have a wealth of hands-on experience which has made them valuable advisors and key leaders.

Keywords – The Silent Generation: *loyalty, reliability and dedication.*

. . . .

Baby Boomers

Born: 1946-1964
[Also known as: Boomers, Hippies, Yuppies, ME Generation, Jones Generation, GenJones, Sandwich Generation]

The Silent Generation began to build a whole new society when they came back from the war. They found work, married and eventually had children - Baby Boomers. In the United States, approximately 79 million babies were born during the Baby Boom. Between 1940 and 1965 the annual number of births in Canada rose from 253 000 in 1940 to 479 000 in 1960. Much of this cohort of nineteen years grew up with Woodstock, the Vietnam War, and John F. Kennedy as president. The baby boom began with the births of children whose conception had been postponed during the Depression. Other factors affected it as well, including more marriages, and more children produced during the marriage. Married and single women born between 1911 and 1912 had an average of 2.9 children, whereas those born between 1929 and 1933 had an average of 3.3. Baby Boomers were a treasured and wanted generation.

*NOTE: The Jones Generation is, truly, the 5th working generation in the current workforce. Born in the late 1960's (at the tail end of the Baby Boom), this generation is the often forgotten because of overlapping.

The tag "Jones Generation" comes from the concept of "keeping up with the Jones'". Though born within the time frame of the Baby Boom, the Jones Generation was in elementary school during Woodstock. They were not old enough to understand the protest at the infamous "Bed-In for Peace" of John Lennon and Yoko Ono.

> Jones Generation is often grouped with the Baby Boomers despite the fact that their experience is distinct. The experience of Jones Generation bridges Baby Boomers and Generation X.
>
> The Jones Generation is the undiscovered demographic. However, for the purposes of this book, the Jones Generation is grouped in with the Baby Boomers.
>
> Grouping the Jones Generation and Baby Boomers together is best explained in the lyrics of The Hollies *"He ain't heavy he's my brother"*.

Most Baby Boomers grew up in traditional nuclear families. They had a working dad and a stay-at-home mom. Mounting prosperity in the home and emergent opportunity in the world at large surrounded them. Unlike the childhood of the Silent Generation, Baby Boomers enjoyed a peaceful and prosperous upbringing.

The Silent Generation hid any personal or professional unhappiness from their Baby Boomer children. The Silent Generation had lived through sacrifice and was intent on giving Baby Boomers a better life. Baby Boomers grew up believing "a better life" has always been a given birthright.

> ### 50's Play list
>
> Elvis Presley releases *"Heartbreak Hotel"*
>
> Nat King Cole's *"Mona Lisa Smile"*
>
> Little Richard's *"Tutti-Frutti"*

Baby Boomers are the first generation of minors who have been marketed to via media channels. Families earned enough to have some disposable income to spend on little luxuries. Radio and (later) television pitched cereals, snacks and toys specifically for the child Baby Boomer market.

All this attention instilled a certain confidence in Baby Boomers that they carried with them into their higher educational experiences and working years. They are comfortable voicing their opinions. They expect public recognition when successful and accomplished.

Baby Boomers came of age in an era of great social change. The assassinations of John F. Kennedy and Martin Luther King Jr. had a profound impact on youth in the Western world. Integration and the women's rights movement also significantly contributed to shaping Baby Boomers. These events prodded Baby Boomers to speak up against authority, to formally protest and engage collectively for a higher cause.

Baby Boomers entered post secondary institutions in droves, resulting in over 40% or baby boomers having some sort of post-secondary education. However, the majority of Baby Boomers still entered the workforce on the ground floor. Baby Boomer aspirations to climb the corporate ladder and create a better life was nurtured through a belief that book smarts, combined with a commitment to the workplace, and an ambitious plan for advancement would eventually lead them into the CEO's chair.

The early Baby Boomer work environment was hierarchal. In addition, there were strict gender and race roles, although women began entering the workplace in large numbers, and by 1965 made up over 30% of the total workforce. Eventually, Baby Boomers would be instrumental in changing the concept of roles in society and also changing the traditional chain of command through their activism.

60's Play list

Aretha Franklin releases *"Respect"*

The Rolling Stones release *"I Can't Get No Satisfaction"*

Summation: Baby Boomers are involved, opinionated workers. They strive for progress and innovation. They are change-makers who "get" the big picture. They are worldly workers who strive for advancement.

Keywords – Baby Boomers: *change, involvement and optimistic.*

. . . . . .

Generation X

Born: 1965-1980
[Also known as: Gen X, Generation Next, X-ers, Xer]

Generation X grew up with the clear understanding that nothing is forever. In their early years, they witnessed the breakdown of the traditional nuclear family. Promises failed and futures were uncertain in the growing years of Generation X (reminiscent of the growing years of the Silent Generation).

> **70's Play list**
>
> The Rolling Stones record
> *"Exile on Main Street"*
>
> Village People sing
> *"YMCA"*
>
> Bruce Springsteen releases
> *"Born to Run"*

With close to 40% percent of gen X-ers growing up in divorced households, Generation X was the first generation to experience visitation rights and alimony. The nuclear family model transformed in the growing years of Generation X, including the renewed existence of the multi-generational household and newly-single-parent families, in concurrence with the "traditional" two parent family model.

Family incomes were one, two or more earnings – to support the family's household, to upgrade the family's lifestyle or for two separate households altogether. Generation X's parents also had the opportunity and ambition to take on projects outside of the home (e.g. a stay-at-home mom could volunteer in the community). In some cases, grandparents moved into the home as caregivers to young children while parents worked outside the home, creating the multi-generational household. Due to the increase in divorce rates, employment and responsibilities outside the home, the concept of "latch-key kids" was born.

Latchkey Generation X-ers had the responsibility of walking themselves (and siblings) home from school, all by themselves, and letting themselves into an empty house. Reminiscent of the days when The Silent Generation children had to fend for themselves while their parents contributed to the war effort, Generation X-ers were often left with little parental supervision once they hit their tweens/teens.

Through this early experience, they honed skills in self-sufficiency. As a result, many members of Generation X have carried with them into the workforce a survivalist attitude.

Generation X saw the end of the Cold War, the U.S. Space Shuttle *Challenger* break apart on live television and the fall of the Berlin wall. They lived through a series of economic crises, such as the 1973 oil crisis, the 1979 energy crisis, the early 1980s recession, Black Monday (1987) and the US savings and loan crisis.

Generation X is a reality-based cohort. They don't "want it all" as they believe "having it all" is unattainable without sacrificing family and home life. From watching Boomers compulsive work habits, Generation X adopted the philosophy that in the pursuit of "it all" something always suffers. As such, Generation X believes a job is just a job. Furthermore, they want a life outside of their job. This attitude can raise flags with employers as a nonchalant. However this detachment is more personality than agenda with Generation X.

In Generation X's opinion, if an organization expects them to work an 80 hour week it means there's a problem with the product, the management or the organization is just plain cheap. Generation X will not work 80 hours a week for a 40-hour a week salary.

Generation X also has a survivor mentality when it comes to priorities. They are quick to sort what information is important and cast everything else in descending order.

Example: Xavier's exam

Xavier studies for his history exam. He scans for the battle dates, the names of the generals and the number of casualties. He skips the sections on military uniform.

In this example, Generation X Xavier scans for information which will be on the history exam. Generation X had educational success due to their strong ability to do keyword searches and prioritize. They brought these talents with them when they entered the workforce.

When Generation X came of age for the labour market, Baby Boomers and the Silent Generation still had firm footing in the "good jobs". Competition in the job market was stiff because of job redundancy and corporate downsizing. Generation X had difficulties finding jobs, as the market was already saturated with experienced workers. Many Gen X-ers returned to post-secondary studies to pursue further certificates and degrees to increase their chances of getting employment.

Generation X owns the concept of non-traditional hours, spaces and locations (i.e. flexible work options) allowing them to "work" on their own schedule. To Generation X time card systems are a thing of the past. Generation X also doesn't consider "casual dress days" perks – comfort at work is a must.

They are unimpressed by formality. In their lifetimes, they have seen too many bigwigs and superstars fall from the pedestals to invest belief in authority. Generation X is more impressed with individuals and organizations that are committed to meaningful work.

Generation X socializes with co-workers more than any generation which preceded them. Moreover, they socialize up and down the corporate ladder (i.e. lunch with a Director, extreme Frisbee with the mail clerk), breaking with the traditional fraternization hierarchy rules of old.

Generation X's resourcefulness, innovation and independence have grown a cohort of innovators. They have launched grassroots organizations and home-based businesses with great success – competing with the "big boys". Generation X has proven you don't need to be +40 years old, wear a tie and work in an office to be successful.

80's Play list

Band-aid recorded:
"Do they know it's Christmas?"

Cyndi Lauper sings *"Girls Just Wanna Have Fun"*

"Ice Ice Baby" by Vanilla Ice

Billy Idol, *Dancing with Myself*

One can consider Generation X to be the notorious "middle child" of the generation family. They were born in between the baby that gets all the attention (Generation Y) and the older sibling who has already accomplished so much (Baby Boomers).

Summation: Generation X grew up with the ability to be resourceful, innovative and multitaskers. They are self-starters who work well independently.

Keywords – Generation X: *self-reliance, multi-tasking and adaptable.*

......

Generation Y

Born: 1981-2000
[Also known as: Millennials, Net Generation, Y-ers,
Yer, Me Generation]

Born to Baby Boomer parents, Generation Y is the most scheduled generation of all time. Baby Boomers wanted to prep their children for success from birth, enrolling them in enriched after-school care, ballet and soccer classes, after school violin study, summer camps and weekend sports teams. The extra-curricular experience has made Generation Y team players comparable to the Silent Generation who also grew up as team players, contributing to the family income as children in the war efforts.

Generation Y was not only a wanted generation but also a very planned-for generation. From birth plans to career goals, Baby Boomers have been hands-on in arranging the lives and events of Generation Y. Consistent with the Baby Boomer experience of getting what they want in the world, Baby Boomers want their children to be well-educated and well on their way to a successful professional life. Through these desires, Baby Boomers have created a generation of kids who viewed themselves as the centre of the universe. Despite their commitment to their jobs Baby Boomer parents' changed their own schedules to accommodate little league soccer games, arranged an active adolescent social calendar and volunteered (by time or money) at their children's school.

Generation Y has also been a highly protected generation. During their growing years, high-end niche markets were created specifically catering to protecting Gen Y-ers. Due to the always looming fear of "stranger danger", Baby Boomer parents sought out indoor playgrounds as destinations for gross motor skills development, safe learning environments, scheduled socialization and independent physical fitness.

Specialized summer camps were created to teach Generation Y even during the school breaks. It provided an opportunity to build on strengths in order to excel in a specific area of interest. Baby Boomers could also be assured that their Generation Y children connected with kids who shared similar interests.

All of this care provision by Baby Boomers to their children has contributed to Generation Y having more of a dependence on their parents than any other generation.

Baby Boomer parenting styles launched terms like Helicopter Parents and Snowplow Parenting. Snowplow parenting is a parenting style in which the parents push any obstacles out of their children's paths – as a snowplow would push snow to clear a pathway. As such, Baby Boomers "take care" of Generation Y from crib to cubical. It is not unheard of for a Baby Boomer parent to set-up, escort and wait in the car for their Generation Y child's job interviews.

> **90's Play list**
>
> Lauryn Hill releases *"The Miseducation of Lauryn Hill"*
>
> Celine Dion has a Titanic hit with *"My Heart Will Go On"*
>
> Spice Girls, a hit in the UK, launch in the US in 1996 with *"Wannabe"*

Generation Y has come from non-traditional homes, where caregivers may be same gender, single parent, two parents, mature parent, or grandparents. Due to their upbringing, Generation Y is comfortable with gender and role bending. One could easily propose a future trend of Generation Y fathers staying home and Generation Y mothers becoming the main financial providers in family households.

Generation Y grew up with educational pre-school cartoons and video games which were designed to develop fine motor skills. They have had the opportunity for long-term formal studies. As such Generation Y is a very sophisticated and knowledgeable generation.

They came of age in the digital era and are a technically savvy, highly connected, generation. Generation Y does not know a world without personal computers, digital cameras or cell phones.

As teens, Generation Y has had the enjoyment of large disposable incomes. They were subsidized by their Baby Boomer parents as well as the availability of part-time jobs. As such, Generation Y amassed from an early age purchasing influence as consumers, generating waves of new forms of marketing Gen Y trends.

To appropriate a quote by Oscar Wilde: many feel that Generation Y knows the price of everything and the value of nothing. Generation Y had a mobile phone by age 13, had travelled overseas numerous times by the time they were 15, and had gone through 4-5 computers by the time they were 18. These experiences have lead to high expectations in their interactions and relationships with their workplaces, parents, and neighborhoods. One could suggest that Generation Y's high level of expectation equals a sense of entitlement. They have grown up to believe that they are entitled to a medal just for showing up at the little league game. They have grown up in an education system where no one fails a grade.

Theirs is a generation of gratification. They amassed high scores on video games, could connect with their social network 24/7 and carried personal entertainment systems so they could never spend a moment bored. Generation Y can enable "on demand" commands to almost all part of their lives, be it social, education or family. Everything is instant. If it's not instantly gratifying, it can be instantly exchanged for something that is.

Yet this is also a civically minded generation, a generation that feels that they can change the world and are taking active steps towards it. Generation Y watched Nelson Mandela's release from Robben Island after almost 30 years of imprisonment. They witnessed two U.S. teens rampage through their high school, killing students and teachers in the Columbine High School Massacre. They experienced 9/11, and the fall of the Twin Towers, on 24 hour news channels. These experiences have lead to Gen Y-ers to volunteer in record numbers, and maintain that level of civic engagement into their adult years. They use social networking sites as a way of organizing around civic and political issues; many have been seasoned fundraisers for a variety of charities since

2000 Play list

U2
releases
"Beautiful Day"

Santana has hits with
"Smooth" and *"Maria Maria"*

Black Eyed Peas record
"Where is the Love?"

their childhood years. They see a problem in the world and don't just throw their hands up in the air about it – they get online, organize, and raise their voices collectively against perceived injustices.

Generation Y entered the workforce with a toolbox filled with education, technical experience and innovative approaches to problem solving. They say accreditation and age alone should no longer be markers for job titles. They believe in goal setting and constant communication. They work well under the guidance of a strong leader – a throw back to their little league/coach days.

Summation: Generation Y grew up believing every child who participates is medal worthy. They are confident and determined to contribute to a team. They could be the near perfect generational marriage: the team orientation of the Silent Generation + the social engagement of Baby Boomers + the multi-tasking savvy of Generation X.

Generation Y keywords: *community-driven, optimistic, choice, connected.*

. . . . . .

	YEARS OF BIRTH	EVENTS and EXPERIENCES	VALUES
THE FOUR GENERATIONS IN THE WORKPLACE			
The Silent Generation	1922-1945	Great Depression New Deal World War II Korean War Pearl Harbor	Loyalty Hardworking Traditional Responsibility before pleasure Conformity Faith in institutions
Baby Boomers	1946-1964	Civil Rights Sexual Revolution Cold War Space travel Assassinations Polio vaccine	Involvement Optimism Team orientation Personal gratification Personal growth
Generation X	1965-1980	Fall of Berlin Wall Watergate Desert Storm Energy Crisis Moon Landing	Self-reliance Diversity Techno literacy Fun and informality Pragmatism
Generation Y	Born: 1981-2000	School shootings Oklahoma City Technology Child focused world 9/11	Community-driven Optimistic Confident Achievement oriented Respect for diversity

TABLE 1 WHO ARE THE FOUR GENERATIONS IN THE NEW GENERATION GAP?

New Generation Gap Timeline

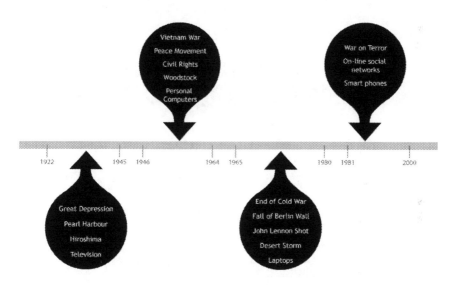

FIGURE 3 NEW GENERATION GAP TIMELINE

NATURE OF A GENERATION GAP

"Crabbed age and youth cannot live together:
Youth is full of pleasance, age is full of care"
--Shakespeare

The generation gap in the workplace can be an enormous source of discord and division. Generational conflict is frustrating, unproductive, and rarely addressed. There are many contributing factors to the nature of a generation gap.

CONTRIBUTING FACTORS TO A GENERATION GAP			
Fear of difference	Shift in values	Economic insecurity	Jealousy
Resentment	Lifestyle changes	Stress	Cultural changes

TABLE 2 CONTRIBUTING FACTORS TO A GENERATION GAP

These factors influence how a team member works and shares information with other members. Emotions play a big part in workplace conflict. Raw feelings can be heavy and burdensome.

Example: Meet Barb

Barb apologized tonight to her husband for being home late because of a big project at work.

Barb is feeling guilty because she had to leave the office early yesterday because her mother fell (they spent 4 hours in emergency).

Barb feels isolated in her department.

Barb grits her teeth every time her colleague Sam calls her *Dear.*

Barb is anxious about coordinating the video conference with the Board of Directors next week.

She is frustrated by her co-worker Yasmin, who in a clear failure of punctuation, includes semi-colons, endash and parenthesis at the end of every e-mail.

Barb feels it her fault for not scheduling her doctor recommended breast exam again this month.

Baby Boomer Barb has to lug around a lot of responsibility and emotion. As do the rest of the generation team members. These emotions can cause pressure which causes resentment and leads to co-worker intolerance. Let's investigate why Baby Boomer Barb is divided from her team.

Silent Generation Sam uses the term *Dear.* Part of Baby Boomer Barb's experience is the women's movement for equal rights. Her identity has been formed as an independent, equal, modern worker. She isn't anyone's *Dear*! To Baby Boomer Barb this term is condescending and belittling.

To Silent Generation Sam – the term *"Dear"* is a tendency from the 1950's era. The experience of the Silent Generation is a patriarchal place of work. In that era, male dominated workforces rarely dealt with women on equal footing in the workplace. The fact that Silent Generation Sam has endured in the workplace demonstrates that he has had the ability to change as times have changed. However, he continues to use *"Dear"* out of sheer habit.

Why does Generation Y Yasmin add a semi-colon, endash and parenthesis combination at the end of every e-mail? It's a winky face of course! ;-) Baby Boomer Barb finds it frustrating. However, to Generation Y Yasmin, it is an olive branch – a sign of friendship. Generation Y is so accustomed to texting that they have brought into the workplace a modern acronymic dialect of written English.

- <3 (heart – as in I love it)
- gr8 (great)
- cul8r (see you later)
- lol (laugh out loud)
- ;-) (winky face)

Texting is quicker then the traditional written word. It lends itself to keying on a portable device as well as a traditional keyboard. It helps convey their message in social networks where they have condensed writing space (i.e. Twitter, Facebook, MySpace). When Generation Y uses their acronymic dialect in communications they are demonstrating their comfort and connection with colleagues.

Generation gaps can be caused by misunderstanding, presuming and emotions. These factors can create an us vs. them conflict in the office. These factors can also be escalated by the pressures of deadlines, projects and personal interactions.

......

Ageism

Ageism can contribute to workplace conflict. It can also cause unease with an individual. Ageism is discrimination of a person or group based on their age (either ascending or descending).

Ageism is a very real barrier in the modern workforce. It can be challenging for younger generations to work with colleagues who are old enough to be their parents – or even grandparents. What about a supervisor that is the same age as your own child?!

Example: **The New Director**

With the retirement of Silent Generation Sam there is to be a new Director in the department. An internal e-mail memo is sent to the team welcoming a Mr. Xavier as the newly hired Director.

❖ NewGen Company is proud to welcome Mr. Xavier to the team! Before joining NewGen Company, Mr. Xavier served as Senior Project Manager for ABC Company where his responsibilities included theme development, marketing and sponsorship development. Mr. Xavier began his career as a Policy Advisor with Green Energy Organization. He went on to serve on the National Green Energy Board (NGEB) in various senior capacities. In 2008, Mr. Xavier received the critically acclaimed Innovator's award.

Monday morning the team met Mr. Xavier. Much to their surprise, Mr. Xavier was a 30-something year old man. He wore jeans and a dress shirt. He apologized in advance for having to leaving early that afternoon - unfortunately it was his day for car pool.

He told the team the clear objective for the meeting was to set the strategic theme for next year's newsletters.

He invited everyone around the table to introduce themselves to him, and as a way of getting to know each other better, invited each team member to share their favourite flavour of ice cream.

How do you think the team will accept the new Director? Boomer Barb may take issue with a senior manager dressed so unceremoniously (perhaps even inappropriately?) for such a senior role. She may feel uncomfortable reporting to someone her junior in years. Generation Y Yasmin might confuse the socializing aspect of the ice cream ice-breaker as an endorsement to treat Xavier as a friend rather than a manager.

The team members are judging Generation X Xavier because of his age. This influences them to jump to quick conclusions about the new Director.

If you were to re-read his biography you would understand that Generation X Xavier has the experience for the job. His qualifications cannot be questioned. Undoubtedly, the ageist determinations of the team will grow insecurity, lack-of-confidence, jealousy and resentment amongst the team.

Let's look at what triggers the presumptions in the first place. Generation X Xavier is a confident, experienced, manager. The majority of Generation X members are known for being unpredictable when it comes to office dress. Generation X Xavier might put on a suit and tie when he meets an external stakeholder. He may wear jeans and a t-shirt mid-week. Generation X Xavier doesn't feel he needs a

Over the last two years, the number of Americans age 55 and older who are still working has climbed by nearly 1.5 million to over 26 million in March, according to the US Bureau of Labor Statistics. The number of people 55 and older who want a job but can't find one has more than doubled over the same period to nearly 1.8 million. Joblessness is lower among older workers than the general labor force, but it's growing much faster.

three-piece suit to do his job – he *needs* his expertise and skills.

Generation X Xavier will leave early for car pool. He will also come in late when he drops his kids off at summer camp. To Generation X Xavier work/life balance is crucial. Yet he's reachable by e-mail, SMS and phone 24/7 thanks to his smart phone device. He doesn't physically need to be in the office to do his job well. Generation X Xavier strongly believes that it's not the amount of hours in-office that proves his success but rather how effectively he carries out his job.

He has absolutely no interest in going to a meeting to discuss the agenda for next meeting. Meetings are about actions, reactions and making things happen. Time is not to be wasted.

Generation X Xavier instigates a team ice breaker by offering an ice cream social. This isn't a hidden message telling the team he's a fun guy. It shows he wants to know his team on a more personal level. Generation X Xavier is good-natured and social. He also understands that a social gathering is a good was to break the ice. He understands making a connection is good business. He treats his employees as he would his clients – with respect, customer service and a smile.

Summation: Through education one can chase away age discrimination. Diversity training, multi-generational workshops and opening the lines of communications are all important tools for a multi-generational leader to use to educate their team. .

......

Current Workplace Structure

The current workplace is saturated with talented workers and prospects which influence the new generation gap. Consider the retirement ceiling – there is no longer a roof in the organizational house. Due to longer life spans and better health the Silent Generation and Baby Boomers have delayed leaving the workforce. They are mentally and physically able to continue on in the office long past the traditional retirement age of 65 years old.

In lieu of "retiring", the Silent Generation and older Baby Boomers are choosing to work a shortened work week, work flexible hours or consult on projects on an as needed basis. Some are even "downsizing" from high ranking titles to supportive roles to keep their hand in the game.

Add in the fact that many members of mature generations must remain in the workforce because of necessity. Baby Boomers are also known as "the sandwich generation" because they are the main care providers to their Silent Generation parents and Generation Y children. Between paying for senior care and post-secondary tuitions – Baby Boomers are sandwiched – emotionally, financially and physically. Some Baby Boomers must remain in the workforce for the sake of their dependents.

> **Water cooler remarks** - The Current Workplace Structure:
> *"Why doesn't she just retire?"*
> *"Who does he think he is?!"*
> *"Where does she think she's going?"*

Summation: The saturated workplace structure grows stress and frustration. Currently, there are four generations in competition for the same jobs. The older generations are still solidly entrenched in the workforce leaving little room to grow for the younger generations. This causes fear and resentment amongst the generations.

......

Hierarchy - Influencers and Expectations

The education and experience of team members influence the new generation gap. The Silent Generation strongly believes they have paid their dues – and that others should too. Remember, that the Silent Generation entered into the workforce where young men started working on the factory floors, middle-aged men were the supervisors and the senior staff had the corner offices.

In the traditional organizational hierarchy everyone followed the chain of command. A worker only interacted with others who were one level up or down from their own level. With experience and age workers would move up the corporate ladder. This influenced the workers' ambitions and expectations of advancement. With advancement in the chain came increased power, clout and autonomy.

The Baby Boomers were a more impatient workforce. They didn't want to wait for the President to retire. They wanted to be the rising star sooner and quicker. It is the Baby Boomers whom modern workers have to thank for the concept of a layered hierarchy in business. This created the possibility for Baby Boomers to climb the corporate ladder with increased speed. Instead of one vice-president there were three. The modern hierarchy has become a chain of command saturated with titles and varying clout; allowing for corporate ladder climbing.

Comparing the traditional and current organizational hierarchies presents a point in understanding the new generation gap. The older generations have experienced, and still expect, the traditional chain of command to play off of age and experience. Though they have less formal education, their immense hands-on experience has been the foundation of their long and prosperous careers.

Younger generations, on the other hand, see through the layers of bureaucracy and designations. Generation X is leery of the chain of command. They have a "been there/done that/have the t-shirt" type of mentality towards hierarchy. Their feeling of being overqualified for their entry-level jobs have lead Generation X to be disillusioned and not intimidated by titles, authority and chain of command.

Many members of Generation X grew tired of the invisible ceilings and red tape of the corporate world. Armed with formal education and advancements in technology, some members of Generation X founded their own organizations. They improved on entrepreneurialism and innovation by growing their own brand on their own terms. Through the X-ers entrepreneurialism, the traditional chain of command was forever changed. The possibility of a 30-something being the head of a prosperous organization was born.

Generation Y respects the chain of command, yet also questions their own place in that chain of command. Generation Y's parents discussed things with them rather than commanded orders. Their Boomer parents have also fêted Generation Y big achievements with great zealousness. Generation Y's formal education invited directed conversation and brainstorming from their educators. They have been treated as celebrated contributors in their family and school lives.

In the office, Generation Y expects a solid mid-level placement in the chain of command regardless of their greenness. They anticipate being included and celebrated because they are participating. Their ego, techno-literacy and formal education accreditation has produced the expectation that they are of great value to the organization.

The influencers of a generation and the expectations created by these influencers can widen the generation gap causing frustration, miscommunication and stress.

......

The Generation Divide – Innate and Created

The generations are separated by years – an innate generation divide. A co-worker can have 10, 20 or 30+ year difference from other team members. There is no way to overcome this innate generation divide. One cannot grow or take away years. (However, one <u>can</u> grow knowledge about working with different generations.) The generations are also divided by misunderstanding. This is a created generation divide. Both types of generational divides can be an enormous source of stress and conflict in the workplace.

Stress

Stress is something faced by all generational groups. While the stressors can be different the effects of stress are felt across the generations. Stress can build frustration, jealousy and insecurity between the generations in the office. It can be a significant contributor to conflict on projects.

Due to the advancements in modern medicine, healthier living and working environments, and more awareness, people can expect to live longer lives than previous working generations. This means that today's older generations need bigger financial nest eggs to provide for their retirement years. Above and beyond planning for the necessities of life, senior generations need to plan for changes in housing, comprehensive health strategies and a higher cost of living in their futures. There are also personal economic goals for travel, contributing to their children's (or grandchildren's) housing/education and activities for social and emotional wellbeing.

Members of the Silent Generation and the front-end of Baby Boomers are having to turn their mind to personal illness, injury, and spousal death. For many

> Regardless of occupation or age, the most commonly cited source of stress was too many demands or hours. That said, however, the likelihood of citing various stress triggers varied somewhat by occupation. According to Statistics Canada, Managers and professionals —particularly in health-related occupations—were significantly more likely to report too many demands or hours compared with workers in manufacturing, processing, primary, or trades occupations.

members of this aging population, they feel that they must remain in the labour market to protect themselves against the pitfalls that might affect their future plans. Gen X-ers and Y-ers are being left to wonder if there will be anything left for them once the current seniors and soon to be retiring Boomers have dipped into government pension plans. Add in the most recent financial losses due to the global economic crisis and many older workers must remain in the workforce to recoup investment losses. Older generations feel the pressure of saving enough money to enable a comfortable retirement lifestyle despite the raising cost of living. Some members of the younger generations may regard aging workers as refusing to go gracefully into that good night – and leave their jobs open for the workers that have been waiting for years to move into those positions. Yet most aging workers feel like they have little choice in staying in their jobs for as long as needed to insure their economic security.

There is also a social pressure amongst the older generations to be a valuable contributor to society, leading many to interpret that contribution as remaining busy in the labour market. In addition, the almost abolition of mandatory retirement has resulted in retirement plans being seen as fluid and based on personal employee circumstances.

Self-employment, part time positions and consultancy are common work arrangements for mature workers. These non-standard positions suggest that though mature workers are interested in reducing their working hours they are not yet detached from the labour market.

Women often face unique stressors in the workplace. Due to a desire for financial freedom, familial financial pressure, increased divorce rates, and a desire for fulfilling careers outside the home, Boomer females entered the workforce in greater numbers than ever imagined by their mother's generation. However, with significant responsibilities outside the home, female workers are often left in the tough position of struggling to find balance between home and work. Currently, Baby Boomer women are sandwiched between being the main care provider to both their aging Silent Generation parents and growing Generation Y children.

Consider the fact that many members of the four working generations are currently experiencing multi-generational living conditions at home. Some members of the more senior generations must move in with their children because of deteriorating health conditions. Moving in with a child can also be a transitional period between residing in one's own home and residing in an elder care facility. Junior generations move back home or continue living at home because of flawed opportunity (job loss, divorce) and/or financial dependency.

In both circumstances of generations moving into a common household there is a lack of privacy, loss of pride and lack of independence that causes stress on the family members and the generations. Members of the Silent Generation and Baby Boomers share a strong sense of independence that be negatively impacted by moving in with their children. Younger generations experience a reduced stigma towards moving in with family. The term boomerang children was inspired by the return of Generations X and Y to the family home (they left but then they came back – hence boomeranging).

> **Example: Generation Y Yasmin – Boomerang**
>
> Yasmin, a student leaves the family home to pursue an engineering degree at university.
>
> Four years later, she takes six months off to volunteer for a non-for-profit organization in Guyana (which looks great on a résumé for life skills, experience working in a culturally diverse environment and building communications skills).
>
> After earning a degree and traveling abroad, the young engineer boomerangs back to the parental home; needing financial support (lodging, food, etc.) while she begins her search for a "real" job and begins her true evolution into independence.

Generation Y incurs increased student debt and longer stays in post-secondary education which contributes to a continued emotional and financial dependence on more established family members. It could be said that 27 years old is the new 17 years old – where the individual is not yet prepared emotionally nor financially to transition from youth to independent adulthood.

> **Example: Generation X Xavier – Boomerang**
>
> Xavier, a lawyer, decides law is not his calling.
>
> The hours, the work environment and the industry cause him stress which impacts his health.
>
> Quitting his job is positive for his overall well-being however it negatively affects his budget.
>
> He must sell his condo and return to his parent's home to restructure his finances.

Some members of Generation X take a step backwards in their career – necessitating them to boomerang home – in order to progress in their quality of life. Other members of Generation X have experienced the breakdown of marital and common-law relationships that has necessitated returning to the parental home. Organizational downsizing and industry failures create job losses that can also factor in Generation X becoming a boomerang child. The high cost of child care and limited availability can provoke a boomerang home for Baby Boomer grandparents to become trusted caregivers while Generation X and Y parents return to the workforce after parental leave.

It is important for a manager to understand and recognize the personal stresses of the respective generations working within their team. These personal stresses can contribute to frustration, lack of communication and aggressive interaction with other colleagues. It is a challenge to leave one's stress at the door. Thus, it happens that personal stress can often be carried into the workplace.

Summation:

The Silent Generation - Stress

- Personal finances (retirement/investments)
- Retirement and lifestyle
- Activity
- Relationships
- Personal health
- Burdening others

Baby Boomer – Stress

- Personal finances (Retirement/investments/disposable income)
- Retirement and lifestyle
- Personal health
- Burdening others
- Relationships
- Caring for aging parents
- Caring for growing children
- Finding balance

Generation X – Stress

- Personal finance (Student debt/home ownership/disposable income)
- Relationships
- Child care
- Professional ambition/growing a career
- Independence/dependence
- Work/life balance

Generation Y – Stress

- Personal finances (Student debt/disposable income)
- Professional ambition/growing a career
- Relationships
- Work/life balance
- Independence/dependence

Example: Xavier's Stress

Xavier resents his co-worker Barb.

Xavier feels jealous of her established career and material wealth. If only she would retire, he could move up in the organization.

If only she would upload her data to the shared drive instead of delivering a paper-copy – he could finish his work and prove his worth.

He is resentful of everything she represents. He brings these negative feelings into the board room and challenges her contributions to projects.

He is terse and sarcastic when he speaks with Barb. Xavier continues his attack at every opportunity.

Barb finally snaps at Xavier in front of a client in retaliation to his war of words.

In this example, Generation X Xavier is creating a divide from Baby Boomer Barb because of his stress. He makes her the "bad guy" for everything he deems wrong in his career. Due to his overpowering stress, he vents his emotion negatively towards his co-worker.

On the other side of this example is Baby Boomer Barb. Baby Boomer Barb works in the office all day, goes home to cook a healthy dinner for her family, then drives to her mom's house to attend to her mother's many medical appointments and prescriptions. Add in Generation X Xavier at the office who is continually confrontational in their group meetings and Baby Boomer Barb is feeling completely overwhelmed.

Summation: Stress can be a powerful contributor to office discord. Specific generational stress along with personal anxieties can create fissures in the framework of your organization's foundation. This can lead to weakness in your team and contribute to generational conflict in the office.

.....

Chapter 3

GENERATIONAL CONFLICT

> *"Whenever you're in conflict with someone, there is one factor that can make the difference between damaging your relationship and deepening it. That factor is attitude."*
> **–William James**

Generational conflict can be an invisible enemy of any organization. It is rarely outwardly voiced but yet inferred in whispers. Triggered by any number of factors - stress, ageism, miscommunication - generational conflict can become a flash point in the workplace. It is essential to investigate conflict and its multiple causes.

In 2009, there were 154,142,000 people in the United States labor force.

Total labor force participation by generation:

- Silent Generation: 6,534,000
- Baby Boomers: 58,710,000
- Generation X: 50,399,000
- Generation Y: 38,499,000

Competition

Consider that in today's workforce there are four generations competing for the same jobs. Each has their own strength: the Silent Generation has experience, Baby Boomers have ideas, Generation X has education and Generation Y has technology.

However, an individual is always susceptible to a competitor possessing a more valuable strength of a specific project.

Example: Filling a Role

The communications department, of an organization, is looking to fill a vacancy for a part-time Media Relations Officer.

Sam mailed his curriculum vitae and cover letter spurned on from reading about the job in the classifieds section of the local newspaper. Sam retired last year from teaching Media Studies at the local college. He is finding retirement boring. He has the know-how to do the job and wants to keep his hand in the industry. He thinks this part-time position is perfect. He has an interview scheduled for Thursday.

Barb has verbally applied despite the fact she is already a full-time Communications Specialist in same organization. She spoke with the hiring Director this morning about the position and conveyed to him that she was a serious candidate. Barb wants to reduce her working hours yet isn't ready to retire just yet. She is already in the organization and has extensive knowledge of the work culture, procedures and clients. She thinks this part-time position is perfect. She and the Director plan to meet tomorrow for a coffee and further discussion.

Xavier has applied through an on-line application via a web-based job site. He is currently a part-time Communications Specialist for a competitor in the same industry. Xavier wants to work under different leadership to expand his knowledge. He hopes to grow into a flexible hour/full time role in the future. In the last year he has been a speaker at two national industry events and has built - on his own time - a database of over 30,000 media contacts worldwide. He thinks this part-time position is perfect. He has an interview scheduled for Monday.

Yasmin has sent her résumé, cover letter and portfolio to the organization's vice president – a colleague of her mentor. Yasmin has been a student member of a national industry organization for two years and actively participates in the organization's mentorship service for guidance and networking. She has recently graduated with honours from a highly competitive post-secondary communications programme. She has grown her portfolio through various volunteer communication roles in well-known companies. She has been profiled in local media as a "Top 10 under 30". Yasmin is fluent in English and French and is functional in Spanish. She has recommendations from many high profile industry leaders – whom she connects with often through social networking tools. She thinks this part-time position is perfect. She has a video conference scheduled for Monday, as she is finishing her internship in the communications department at the European Space Agency in Germany.

Who will fill the role as the part-time Media Relations Officer? Each candidate is strongly qualified, in their own way. Silent Generation Sam has the expert training in the field and could make a valuable knowledge sharing contribution. Baby Boomer Barb has experience in the organization and could seamlessly transition into the role. Generation X Xavier is known in the industry and the organization could take advantage of his knowledge of new technologies. Generation Y Yasmin has ambition backed by education and language – the organization could shape her career to the benefit of both.

In 2009, there were 18,368,800 people in the Canadian labour force.

Total labor force participation by generation:
- Silent Generation: 460,000
- Baby Boomers: 6,988,700
- Generation X: 6,079,000
- Generation Y: 4,841,100

The competition for jobs can create anxiety and animosity amongst the generations. For example, how will Baby Boomer Barb react if she is not chosen but is in the department to witness Silent Generation

Sam become the Media Relations Officer. She may be resentful that she didn't get the wanted part-time position. She may feel enmity towards working with Silent Generation Sam on projects. Such issues can lead to conflict in the workplace.

.....

Financial Tensions

All four generations in the workplace are under financial pressures, although for varying reasons.

> ### Example: Making Quota
>
> *Each team member of the New Product department will receive a bonus if the department hits their quota target. If they exceed their quota they will receive a 10% increase on their bonuses.*
>
> Barb, Xavier and Yasmin would all like to exceed the quota this year, and each for different reasons.
>
> Barb wants to invest the proceeds in a safe retirement fund. Her previous team made quota every year and she expects to continue her streak.
>
> Xavier needs to put the bonus against a line of credit he took out this year to finance renovating the unfinished basement into a home office and playroom. Making the quota will also be a positive addition to his résumé.
>
> Yasmin is drowning in student debt and the bonus will help her keep her head above water. Having the quota in her back pocket will prove her abilities to management.
>
> However, the team is short of meeting their goal thus far. Barb is frustrated by Yasmin – as she is constantly on her blackberry rather than speaking with IT about the project. *Why is she so lazy?*

Xavier is bothered by Barb – who hasn't updated the product list since last month despite the scheduled launch of new products. *What's her problem?*

Yasmin is annoyed by both Barb and Xavier. She tries to SMS Barb in meetings – but Barb never answers. She asks Xavier how to import a pivot table into her spreadsheet – but he just tells her to use the help module instead of talking her though it. *Why is she so stuck-up? Why is he so un-helpful?*

They don't make the quota. The team has hit a boiling point. They don't even want to sit in the same room together. Each teammate blames the others for their loss.

In this example, each teammate is driven by their own personal motivations to make quota. Instead of joining together the team falls apart. Each of the three teammates feels the burden of competition at varying levels. Baby Boomer Barb is competing for a better retirement lifestyle. Generation X Xavier is competing for a better living arrangement. Generation Y Yasmin is competing to further her career. Their personal motivators take precedence over the team objective.

Each of the teammates is making assumptions about the others. Baby Boomer Barb is presuming that Generation Y Yasmin is connecting with friends on her blackberry when she may in fact be connecting with other co-workers. To Generation Y social networking sites are not just for play they are also for work, education, and personal life. Gen Y workers have a different sense of the value of social network sites – networking is a constant objective, and relationships with co-workers may be casually defined as both one of colleagues and friends if they have connected on sites such as Facebook or Twitter. For most Gen Y-ers social networks seem like a more effective way of communicating, as users can chime in in real time reducing time wasted between individual e-mails and responses.

Generation X Xavier assumes Baby Boomer Barb has a problem updating the list – but perhaps the problem has nothing to do with

Baby Boomer Barb. Perhaps the list cannot be updated as there is no new valuable information to add at this point. There could have been an unforeseen challenge with the scheduled launch or with the new products themselves. Barb has proven throughout her career that an organized approach to projects reduces risk and is a more effective way of working.

Generation Y Yasmin presumes Xavier knows how to import a pivot table. Yet, being a thirty-something-mobile-phone-carrying-guy doesn't make him an expert on spreadsheet tools. He may be advising her to use the help module of the application because that is the most effective way to learn.

Yasmin presumes Barb doesn't answer her SMS because she is snobbish. However, Barb may feel it is rude to answer an SMS when she is participating in a face-to-face meeting. To Baby Boomer Barb, it is proper business etiquette to provide full focus on the meeting and prioritize on the task at hand.

The breakdown of the team (and missing the mark of their objective) was because the team made assumptions about each other, lacked understanding, and did not communicate effectively.

......

Generational Tensions

It is a reality that in today's modern office, title no longer reflects education or experience. This can contribute to cynicism and tension - especially amongst the Silent Generation and to some extent, Baby Boomers who hold dear to the philosophy of paying dues in the hierarchy system.

> **Example: The Consultant**
>
> *The organization has hired the expertise of a Youth Engagement Specialist named Yasmin, to consult on this year's marketing plan.*

Yasmin is in her early twenties and highly motivated. Upper management decides to pull in team members from other projects to support Yasmin in her consultations.

Sam feels uncomfortable being commanded by someone old enough to be his granddaughter. It goes against his experience with hierarchy, authority and tradition. He stays quiet in meetings and answers only when directly asked to.

Barb questions Yasmin on every point. Barb has a hard time digesting Yasmin's "expertise". Barb interacts daily with members of Yasmin's generation; they cut her grass, play basketball with her sons, and swipe her pass at the gym. Barb doesn't have faith that someone so young should have such a high level of responsibility. She brings her laptop to meetings and pivots the screen to show the team her research.

Xavier notes through discussions and communications that Yasmin has sound insight into the youth demographic. She is dynamic. Her ideas are innovative. He feels a pit in the bottom of his stomach. *She'll replace me.* Xavier has just returned from parental leave and as such is not up to speed on the latest trends. He volunteers to take on work above and beyond his role to ensure his place on the team.

In this example, one can note many generational tensions. Silent Generation Sam is uneasy. Baby Boomer Barb does not have confidence in upper management's decision or in the expertise of the consultant. Generation X Xavier feels out-of-date and insecure about his role. These tensions can sabotage the team.

Tensions are further compounded by attitude, overconfidence and insecurity. In the above example, Sam's attitude about age influences his view of Yasmin. Barb's concerns makes her seem abrasive during meetings. Xavier is insecure about his value to the organization.

These elements fuel the fires of the *"They don't know/I know"* circular debate. Round and round workers debate how much they know and how little another co-worker knows…all the while nothing gets done.

One could surmise that the *"They don't know/I know"* circular debate is a sort of self-preservation in the office. It pads the ego. It calms insecurities about the potential truth -- that one does not, in fact, know it all. This is hard to digest by some established generations who have built their reputations and careers by being experts on their jobs.

Truth-be-told, when was the last time you confessed you didn't know something? It's a difficult thing to do. The Silent Generation and Baby Boomers do not want to lose face. Generation X and Generation Y are concerned that they will look inept. The preservation instinct of a worker is very strong whether one is standing on the production line, sitting in a cubical or occupying the corner office.

It can be suggested that the younger generations think they know it all and the mature generations believe they have seen it all. This is another circular debate which grows tension. The *"I-know-more-than-you"* contest. In the above example, Baby Boomer Barb is convinced that she knows more than Generation Y Yasmin – and even – upper management. Yet, our approach to our work, should be much along the lines of: we always have something to learn, and hopefully, something to impart. If we can see ourselves as both the mentor and the mentee in multiple relationships across the workplace, then we'll cultivate an environment of creative questioning and lifelong learning.

Think about the generations are your team. Are there tensions? Or is something, like technology, making them tense?

……

Technology

Remember back to the preface when it was presented that one should not generalize about the generations? One cannot (and should not) stereotype an individual's skills because of the overall strength or weakness of a generation.

There are members of Generation Y who do not know how to use a formula in a spreadsheet though they have grown up in a digital world. Some members of Generation X cannot configure a wireless router despite the fact they use a laptop on a daily basis. Some Baby Boomers are masters of smart phone devices but cannot programme the family's PVR. Some members of the Silent Generation prefer e-mail as a means of communication despite the fact that e-mail is a tool born two generations after the Silent Generation entered the workforce. A leader should not underestimate (or overestimate) the technology knowledge of a generation. Assumptions cultivate tension, insecurity and conflict within one's team.

Technology can make work more collaborative but can also foster competition. This is an across-the-board issue of the four working generations. While one individual may excel at application, another individual may stumble causing insecurity and anxiety to the less technology-savvy worker. Colleagues may feel at a disadvantage due to technological weakness. They may not be able to contribute to the extent they are able (or willing) because of technical limitations. They may be excluded from updates, team work and project management because of it. A solution to overcoming the invisible barriers of technology is to promote digital learning development through life-long learning and mentorship.

> 97% of US college-age students own a computer, 94% own a cell phone, and 56% own a MP3 player.

Harnessing the power of technology along with the innovation of an individual creates a strong tool for an organization. It allows for faster process. It contributes to team building. It deconstructs departmental inclinations to ownership and boundaries. There should be a focus on partnering for new hires to adapt to the technology in an organization. Partnering is also advised for all generations when new digital tools are introduced to the department. This allows for swapping tips, peer-to-peer support, brainstorming and team development.

When introducing new digital tools and policies, management should keep in mind that change can be difficult to accept to some individuals (no matter the generation). Increased time should be projected for orientation and training. Instruction for all generations should be done with respect acknowledging personal experience.

It is valuable to an organization to consider what digital tools the generations are currently using in their daily lives both inside and outside the office. A collaborative culture can be supported by using the everyday digital tools that the generations are already using. This makes the introduction of digital collaboration more of a grassroots movement than a boardroom decision. If the generations already have some experience with a digital tool they have greater confidence and more authority. They are also equipped to share/train/mentor others on those very applications.

Technology also offers added-value to an organization's general ledger. Consider the cost of setting up an in-person seminar; you need to have space, equipment, seating and perhaps food/drink (depending on the length of the seminar). An attendee requires transportation and travel time. This all creates cost.

Audio conference calls, video conference calls, webinars, chat rooms, white boards, on-line meeting and social networks are cost reduction centres in terms of budget. In some circumstances, digital meetings only require a computer, webcam, microphone an internet connection and the persons involved. Plus, it is zero-carbon emissions so you are not only reducing a cost centre but also demonstrating your organization's commitment to environmentally responsible business operations.

Technology Use By The Generations

The Silent Generation	Baby Boomers
Work (Internet, e-mail) Information: (news, health)	Information (news, health) Work (Internet, e-mail, PIN, smart devices, video conferencing) Social (social networks) Shopping (groceries, gifts)
Generation X	**Generation Y**
Entertainment (music, movies, games) Information (news, health, events, rss feeds, industry updates, advice, GPS) Work (Internet, e-mail, smart devices, video conferencing, webinars, job search) Social (social networks, SMS, blogs, vlogs, podcasts, wikis, e-vites) Shopping (groceries, gifts, clothing, activity registration, vacations) Financial (send money, pay bills, bank transfers)	Entertainment (music, movies, games) Information (news, events, GPS, rss feeds, alerts, collaboration tools, assignment research) Work (Internet, e-mail, smart devices, video conferencing, webinars, job search) Social (social networks, SMS, chat, forums, blogs, vlogs, podcasts, wikis, e-vites, virtual world) Shopping (groceries, clothing, activity registrations, vacations) Financial (send money, pay bills, bank transfers)

FIGURE 4 TECHNOLOGY USE BY THE GENERATIONS

What can an organization do to build on the digital tools that the generations already use in their everyday life? One can start a bottom-up communications framework for the organization. As previously discussed, the front-line troops of the organization are the employees - not upper management. Employees have a wealth of knowledge about customers, services, products and procedures. If an organization fosters a collaborative culture you can harness this knowledge. You can then use collaborative, communicative technology to your advantage for authentic, faster, innovation. At the same time, it empowers the four working generations.

> **Example: Virtual Whiteboard**
>
> *The Environmental Committee has raised a concern about the saturation of paper in the office. Xavier has e-mailed the team manager asking for an addition to the next team meeting agenda… Office Waste.*
>
> At the weekly team meeting, the manager is impressed to see that this issue is important to all members of the team. This presents an ideal opportunity for collaboration.
>
> Immediate, improvisational brainstorming occurs in the team meeting (which Barb loves) on how to tackle the challenge of office waste. The team members deliberate on sources of waste and solutions. The meeting far exceeds its allocated time. There is a general consensus that office waste should be addressed.
>
> Xavier, who brought the idea to the table, and Barb, volunteer to take on the coordination of this task. With the help of the IT department an inter-office virtual white board is set up.

A virtual whiteboard is a digitally-based collaborative tool which provides a real time space for brainstorming with colleagues.

Sam has never used a virtual whiteboard. He requires some training on the tool. However, he is willing to give the whiteboard a try because he wants to contribute to the project and help the team.

The other members of the team; in Generation X and Y are accustomed to using social networking tools (writing on walls) and chat forums. Although neither had used one in the workplace before, both are very comfortable with the concept of the whiteboard.

Once the whiteboard goes live there is a surge of anonymous suggestions on how to solve the office waste problem.

- *"There are too many drafts of documents in circulation. It's a waste of paper and confuses me!"*

→ *"We should set up a wiki for that!"*

- *"Driving to off-site meetings, with all my files, is a complete pain. I lose 45 minutes of potential working time because of the commute. It's a waste of my time. Plus, with the cost of gas - it costs the organization $$."*

→ *"Couldn't we just conference call? e-mail the agenda and documents ahead of time for a c.c.? Saves time, money and sanity."*

→ *"e-mail more – photocopy less – it's better for the environment anyway!"*

→ *"I don't have a far commute but I know others do. If a video/audio conference element were available - I'm sure they would appreciate not having to spend any more time in transit."*

- *"Does HR really need a paper-based copy of my vacation request?"*

→ *"I second that! Plus, it takes FOREVER to get confirmation of receipt. Can't we just switch to on-line forms?"*

The volunteer coordinators, Xavier and Barb, have moderated the white board to ensure the comments were respectful and on-topic. The virtual whiteboard has successfully identified specific areas of waste. In addition, the team has been able to collaborate on how to eradicate the problem areas.

Upper management is impressed by the viral route of the collaboration. As coordinators, Barb and Xavier realize that the suggestions suggest that the team would be attracted to a Green Office Initiative. They bring this realization to management supported by the data of the whiteboard.

Management agrees and approves.

Steps are made to put the suggestions in action.

A Green Office Initiative puts into practice office procedures which are ethical, sustainable and respectful to the environment.

In the above example, we can see how moderated collaboration can take advantage of the strengths of the generations. Though training time was needed by the mature generation members at the beginning - the organization eventually had a return on investment with Silent Generation Sam's contribution.

The organization was able to tap into the mature generation's experience and the younger generation's innovation to identify and solve problems. This was bottom-up communication, where front life staff identified the challenges and communicated these challenges to all levels of the organization.

In addition, the team members spontaneously suggested cost-saving-centres to the organization and work/life balance solutions for their teammates. There is not just loyalty to one's physical team but to other stakeholders beyond the cubical.

Ignorance and fear of the unknown hurt digital collaboration. Moderation is often required to eradicate negative comments (which support negative power). It is important, as it was done in the above example, to make clear the objective in a collaborative project.

The Main Objectives in Digital Collaboration

1. Sharing knowledge/experience
2. Identifying challenges
3. Brainstorming
4. Devising solutions

Is Brainstorming effective?

Brainstorming can seem like a waste of time when it's not done effectively. Even though something may be called a brainstorming session there should still be an organized approach to it – background documents prepared, a series of guiding questions, a facilitated discussion. Goals should be set for any brainstorming session, and follow up procedures set up.

Digital collaboration is a great way to keep stakeholders in the loop. Due to lack of digital experience, some team members may experience anxiety, fear and rejection of the "new" technology. It is important for an effective manager to recognize and appreciate the stress of new technologies (especially amongst the mature generations). One should set up a support centre, including training and mentoring on new tools as a resource for the generations.

Some examples of digital collaboration tools for the workplace include: wikis, blogs, vlogs, forums, chat, walls, whiteboards and shared drives. These tools can be attractive to the Silent Generation and Baby Boomers as they use the formal typed word to convey communication. Generation X and Generation Y can be attracted to the speed, authenticity and interaction elements of the tools.

Paper-based memorandums and e-mail attachments simply *push information* back and forth. When there are changes/edits to information contained in those two communication platforms there is the risk of circulating versions 1, 2 and 3 of a document simultaneously. This misinformation can be confusing and potentially embarrassing to an organization.

However, digital collaboration tools *pull information.* There are no geographical boundaries to the documents (attractive for Baby Boomers and Generation X-ers who telecommute). Real time changes can be made to the document – updating/editing/changing information. This results in an up-to-date document which keeps teammates "in the know" at all times.

Technology can create a buzz amongst the generations. It can become a common thread between teammates; fostering team building and relationships. Technology also works with the strengths of the generations - the Silent Generation has valuable experience to share with the team, Baby Boomers want their ideas heard, Generation X wants to streamline and Generation Y is socially networked by nature.

Summation: Collaboration offers the opportunity to work across hierarchical structures and socialize with others in the organization. It brings teammates together - sharing knowledge and experience - with a common objective. This is a step towards Bridging the Generation Gap.

......

Chapter 4

BRIDGING THE GENERATION GAP

> *"Tell me and I will forget. Show me and I may remember. Involve me and I will understand. "*
> *-- Reputed to have been said by Confucius*

By involving the team, you foster an environment of engagement and encouragement that will bring about productivity and innovation. From the Silent Generation down to Generation Y – all generations want to be involved. Involvement is motivational. Involvement recognizes ability. Involvement is confidence building.

The key to involving a multi-generational team is to have a strong leader. This leader should have in their toolbox management and communications styles specific to working with individuals of diverse background. A static management style is ineffective with a multi-generational team. There is no one-way-fits-all solution to leading a department with different generational members. The most effective strategy is to adopt a fluid management style which can change as change requires (see page 60). Fluid management of the four working generations will bridge the divide, deescalate conflict and promote efficiency.

WHAT DO THE GENERATIONS WANT IN A LEADER?...	
The Silent Generation	The Silent Generation wants a leader to be an authority in the industry. The Silent Generation wants a leader who possesses positional authority. They want a leader who has a vision and plan – for the good of the organization.
Baby Boomers	Baby Boomers want a leader to be a guide. They want a leader to be knowledgeable and non-authoritarian. Baby Boomers want to be part of the decision making process with a leader. They want a leader to be a listener with action.
Generation X	Generation X wants a leader to be a mentor. Generation X wants a leader to enhance their professional development and marketability. They are looking for a leader who is fair and flexible to their career plans.
Generation Y	Generation Y wants a leader to be a coach. Generation Y wants feedback and skills development from a leader. They want a leader to help make their lives more meaningful. They want a leader who will help them be the best.

TABLE 3 WHAT DO THE GENERATIONS WANT IN A LEADER?

Leadership

Mature generations are attracted to leadership that has focus, manages effectively and promotes success. Younger generations gravitate towards leadership that is dynamic, innovative and responsible. It is valuable to offer to your organization's leadership the opportunity to attend a key note address or workshop on "Managing and Motivating Multiple Generations". Through a professional development prospect such as this management can understand the generations, bridge the generation gap and create a productive team using the specific strengths of each generation. It can also help a leader identify team challenges and define objectives to work towards.

Leadership, in a multi-generational organization should lead by example. Graciousness, respect and inclusion of diversity should be demonstrated and supported in every level of operations.

> **33% of executive's time is spent responding to crises or problems.**
>
> 66% of business leaders say they are more aggressively educating employees on their role in delivering on the value proposition.
>
> 69% of business leaders say it's important to have a mentor.

Example: Choosing Teams

Project Manager Xavier must choose a team to brainstorm concepts for a new word-of-mouth initiative.

Xavier invites Sam and Barb onto the team. He casually tells them that he hasn't included Yasmin because she lacks experience.

Barb agrees and adds that Yasmin is too young for such a big project. Barb says that she had given Yasmin a stack of files to alphabetize and she struggled with just that.

Sam nods in silence.

In the above example, it is Generation X Xavier, the team leader who creates the divide within his workplace. He purposefully excludes an individual based on their perceived inexperience. He performed a near complete what NOT to do checklist of working with multiple generations - ageism, lack of confidence, presumption and sabotage. By reporting his bias to other team members he knowingly – or – un-knowingly gives permission to the team to create generational divides themselves.

Baby Boomer Barb agrees with her team leader. Most workers would find it challenging to speak up against a manager's decision. It is easier to agree. In addition, if you agree with your manager and you then provide an example of the righteousness of the agreed upon decision – well, it makes you look better…right?

Baby Boomer Barb adds on that Generation Y Yasmin experienced challenges with the simple task of alphabetization that further supported Generation X Xavier's opinion on Generation Y Yasmin. Silent Generation Sam says nothing. He follows the decisions of his leader without question. However, he is a witness to the generational divide.

What Generation X Xavier *should* have done is full inclusion on the project. He *should* have set a standard for respect, regardless of years of experience, recognizing that potential and desire to contribute is an important asset in any employee. He should have taken this new project as an opportunity for mentoring and knowledge transfer.

A leader of a multi-generational workforce must realize that whether casually or formally your team is always listening. Your remarks, however off-the-cuff, set the standard for the office code of conduct.

Quite often, the situation arises when a leader will be younger than one or more of the team members. As a leader, you must be respectful of generational differences, but still acknowledge a need to work cohesively. You must respect the contributions of all of the generations. Most importantly a leader should not be intimidated by the potential of others, but rather see that potential as an opportunity for the entire team to excel.

> *Lead with respect – communicate with respect – expect respect in return.*

Trust

Trust is an essential quality to any healthy relationship. Ultimately, all generations will want to trust in their organizations, and be trusted by the organization. However, different generations bestow trust in different ways. The Silent Generation will place automatic trust in a leader with a long résumé of experience and education. Their trust is unquestioning and whole-hearted in an organization's leadership. Remember, they entered a very autocratic workforce and still carry with them a sense of duty to authority.

Example: Sam's Trust

Sam will follow the recommendations from the Board of Directors because he has always followed the recommendations from the Board. Despite the fact that the Board Membership has changed over the years, to Sam, the entity or role of the board remains steadfast.

Baby Boomers will trust a leader with a list of accomplishments and awards. Baby Boomers respect recognition – they even strive towards it themselves. However, should a leader falter…Baby Boomers are quick revoke their trust.

Example: Barb's Trust

Barb followed the recommendations from the Board of Directors until Mr. X came aboard. Mr. X makes decisions based on the general ledger and not on the client experience which infuriates Barb. She has no interest in what the Board recommends or doesn't recommend.

Generation X and Generation Y will trust a leader who has succeeded in business with innovation. To the younger generations, innovation means progress, efficiency and meaning.

> **Example: Xavier and Yasmin's Trust**
>
> Xavier and Yasmin didn't pay much attention to the recommendations of the Board of Directors until Ms. Y suggested a Green Work initiative. Ms. Y was a new Board member who had excellent results in a competing organization with creating an environmentally friendly workplace. It cut costs, reduced waste and decreased the number of employee sick days because the office environment was "greener".
>
> Xavier and Yasmin trust the Board because they trust Ms. Y.

Trust is not just a matter of credentials. You must earn the trust of the team by your actions, intentions and reactions. A leader should have an over-all understanding of the generations in the office. Understanding helps identify cultural experience, influencers and expectations of all team members.

Credibility is also an intrinsicly linked to trust. As a responsible leader, you shouldn't just talk to hear yourself speak. You need to actively listen to the concerns of your underlings and take action accordingly. If an employee thinks her concerns fall on deaf ears, her motivation is affected, which affects her work production, which then affects the team as a whole.

> When workplace studies ask about satisfaction and trust, it turns out that trust is enormously highly correlated with life satisfaction. Just moving up one point on a ten-point scale of trust in your management has the life satisfaction equivalence of a one-third increase in income.

Trust is an important tool which has two heads. On the one end, employees should feel an invested trust in their team leader. This builds confidence at all steps – from administrative details to final outcomes agreements. On the other head, the team leader should appear to reciprocate confidence in the team. This builds confidence in working relationships and is motivational. However, some generations confuse trust and clarity.

Members of the Silent Generation and Baby Boomers may confuse "questioning" with a lack of trust.

Example: Questioning

Vice-President Xavier questions Barb about the data she contributed to the project analysis.

He asks: *"Is this the most recent data?"*

Barb wonders: *"Is Xavier questioning my competency? Doesn't he trust me?!"*

To Baby Boomer Barb questioning demonstrates lack of confidence. Mature employees have a weak spot when it comes to questions. They arouse suspicion. They imply a missed mark. But for Generation X Xavier the question is not a strike at confidence at all but rather a true query of clarity.

Generation X and Y grew up surrounded by questions. Through education and experience they have been invited to inquire and investigate. To the younger generations questions are for greater knowledge. They provide information. For Generation X Xavier asking about data is simply a matter of illumination. It is not a personal or professional dig at aptitude.

Generations imply different meanings from something as simple as a question. This can affect the impression of how trusted a team member feels. It can affect how much trust a team member will instill in other colleagues.

> **Blessed is the generation in which the old listen to the young; And doubly blessed is the generation in which the young listen to the old.**
> **-   Old Adage**

Zero-tolerance Prejudice Policy

A progressive workplace will have a zero-tolerance policy when it comes to disrespect in the office. No matter the project, communication or conflict there should always be respect towards each individual team member.

This means that slurs regarding gender, age, race, religion and/or sexuality are absolutely not tolerated. This policy should be formal, documented and well communicated throughout the office.

By establishing a zero-tolerance prejudice policy in an office, one can deescalate potential conflict before it arises. The policy becomes a code of conduct for all staff, including those in the most senior of positions.

......

Focus

Organization and focus go hand in hand. It is important for managers to be organized in their thought, communications and agendas. Conflict arises with miscommunication. With organization and solid communication, team members will have understanding of their responsibilities and expectations of the responsibilities of others.

The main objectives in focusing a multi-generational team

- What is our mandate?
- What is the goal of the team/project?
- What needs to happen to get there?
- Who needs to be involved (internal)?
- Who needs to be involved (external)?
- What is the timeline?

Across the board, all four generations in the current workforce are attracted to leadership/organizations with a strong sense of focus. Focus creates an environment of productivity with potential for accomplishment.

......

Conflict Management

A leader of a multi-generational workforce works to meld the generations into a productive team. At times, this means managing intergenerational conflicts. It is of value to consider the attitudes of the different generations regarding conflict decision.

The Silent Generation looks to upper management for conflict resolution. To this generation, the final word comes from the corner office. The boss makes the decision about resolving a matter and they follow.

Baby Boomers are more fluid with how they perceive and manage conflict in the workplace. They are not shy to voice their opinions. Baby Boomers experienced the social upheaval of the 1960s and 1970s, when the status quo was challenged, and massive movements for change – from the civil rights movement to the anti-war movement to the women's rights movement – taught them that people power can overturn long standing institutions and rules. They may go along with a decision on conflict resolution - if they agree with it.

Members of Generation X are disengaged with conflict management. They have opinions but don't feel their opinions matter in the conflict resolution. Generation X may follow a decision…but after-office-hours they will be updating their résumé.

Generation Y are similar to the Silent Generation in that they look to authority to resolve conflict. They have grown up with snowplow parents and little league coaches who have decided their conflicts - on and off the playing field. In the workplace, Generation Y expects management to go to bat for them. Traditionally, the mature generations follow written decisions handed down by management.

Younger generations respond well to informal, verbal, one-on-one sessions to guide conflict de-escalation. [Note: younger generations are socially-networked-by-nature and may casually stir the pot over – in their network – should they disagree with conflict decisions]

When it comes to intergenerational conflict management it is important for a leader to remember that all employees matter-regardless of their experience or age. It is important for a leader to be a neutral party with conflict management.

Conflict management is always situationally varied. At times, the generations complement each other and at others they conflict. The best practice is to take on a *fluid management style* which motivates the generations and engages them in work. However, conflict does arise despite a leader's best efforts.

> Research shows that 60-80% of all difficulties in organizations stem from strained relationships between employees, not from deficits in individual employee's skill or motivation.

It is advisable to put out fires before they become explosive hazards to the team. This is called conflict de-escalation. A multi-generational leader should consider what is the root cause of the conflict at hand? Is the generational conflict because of a people or a procedure breakdown?

Should the failure be people based then a manager must confront the conflict without bias. An effective leader must be impartial yet gracious. You must take the time to meet with the respective disputing parties one-on-one; listening to their concerns and challenges. It is important to have the confidence of your employee so that they will feel comfortable to share their conflict knowing there will be no backlash or blacklisting from upper management in the organization.

It is ok as a manger to be human, and to remember that employees are bringing their own life happenings into the workplace – a new baby, an elderly parent, a flooded basement, the list of day-to-day frustrations that we must all cope with is long. Empathy is not a form of favouritism. It means you can identify with the experience. In some circumstances it means that you may want to offer support, or be flexible with your expectations during a difficult period of time in someone's life.

And while both personal and professional tensions may lead to periods of conflict in the workplace, that conflict does not mean that you, or your staff, need to pick sides. All serious conflicts should be treated with respect and neutrality. Conflict should be addressed according to a process that has been determined by the organization with input from staff.

The Silent Generation and Baby Boomers have the experience to be able to compare procedures – both positively and negatively. Generation X and Generation Y love to troubleshoot and come up with solutions.

It is valuable to note that change to procedure can often give birth to conflict. By nature, some people, are resistant to change (imposed or requested). This is because of personality, experience or situation.

> **Water cooler remarks** – Conflict Management – Fear of Change:
>
> *"If it ain't broke – don't fix it!"*
>
> *"The more things change – the more they stay the same."*
>
> *"Are they trying to re-invent the wheel?"*

Introduce change slowly to de-escalate potential conflict. Provide clear communication about the objective for the change. Most individuals can accept change better if they understand the reasoning for the change.

A leader of a multi-generational team should be able to manage conflict with understanding, clear communication and decision-making.

However, a leader should never be an overpaid, overqualified, babysitter. You should not have sit in on meetings to ensure conflicting workers "play nice". You should not have to continually praise disgruntled workers for basic performance just to get them motivated. As a leader, does your job profile or salary reflect babysitting services? Probably not.

On the other hand, does your employee's job profile or salary reflect that they require to be babysat? Are they competent or do they require around-the-clock-care-giving? Competency has *nothing* to do with age or generation; however, it has *everything* to do with attitude and experience. It is a leader's role to distinguish the difference.

A multi-generational leader must pilot, focus and harness the strengths of employees. The best practice for doing this is to have a four tiered *fluid management style* approach.

The Ladder of Inference

The Ladder of Inference is a model of how people process information (presented in *Overcoming Organizational Defenses* by Chris Argyris and *The Fifth Discipline Field Book* by Peter Senge).

Picture a ladder.... we begin at the base with real data and experience, the kind that would be captured by a secret camera. The first rung of the ladder represents a set of selected data and experience that we pay attention to. This is the data or experiences we select because of our past experiences, values, or beliefs. We also may overlook any data that doesn't match what we 'expect' to see.

Going up another rung of the ladder, we then affix meaning to what we have selected to see, and develop assumptions (third rung). These assumptions then become the basis for our conclusions (fourth rung). We then finally develop beliefs (fifth rung) or reinforce those we already had. These beliefs then form the basis of our actions (top of the ladder), which ultimately create additional real data and experience.

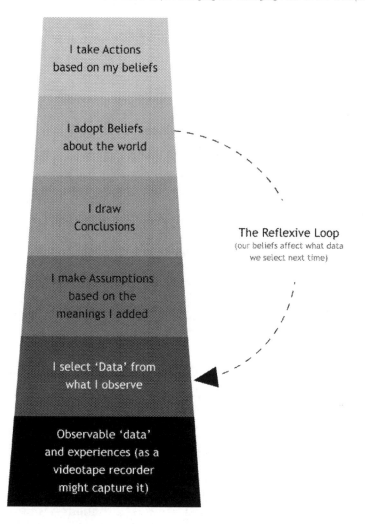

FIGURE 5- CHRIS ARGYRIS' LADDER OF INFERENCE ADAPTED FROM PETER SENGE'S 5TH DISCIPLINE FIELDBOOK

Example: Assuming Negative Intention

Baby Boomer Barb was presenting to her team about the proposed project launch timeline for the coming year. She speaks enthusiastically about the project goals and outcomes, and outlines how the timeline dates have been chosen.

While presenting Barb notices several of her colleagues seem disinterested. Silent Generation Sam was always looking in her direction but has not asked any questions or made any comments. Generation X Xavier asks to see the proposed timeline in writing rather than talking about it. Generation Y Yasmin was playing on her blackberry during the entire presentation. Barb feels Yasmin, Sam and Xavier were obviously not listening. In fact, they probably think that she is incapable of making a sound timeline. Now that Barb thinks about it, Sam, Xavier and Yasmin have never liked any of her ideas. Clearly, they are out to discredit her as project manager. By the time Barb returns to her seat, she has made a decision. She is not going to include anything in her project report to explain the timeline. Sam, Xavier and Yasmin would just take exception to it anyway and use it against Barb.

In those few seconds before she has taken her seat, Barb has climbed up what Chris Argyris calls a "ladder of inference," – a common mental pathway of increasing abstraction, often leading to misguided beliefs. How we view the world and how we act, influences what we select to "see," the interpretations we make and the conclusions we draw. This then leads us to act in ways that produce results that usually reinforce the assumptions we made. Barb started with observable data (Xavier's request for more information), selected some details about Yasmin's behaviour (her apparent non-stop texting), moved rapidly up to some assumptions about her colleagues' current state of interest (they are bored with Barb's presentation!), added her own assumptions about the environment (everybody was in a rush for her to finish) and concluded that in general her colleagues were not interested in what Barb had to say. Therefore as she reaches the top of the ladder she chooses to withhold information.

Of course, adding meaning or making conclusions is a common way that we interact in our relationships with colleagues, family members and friends. However, we can improve our communications through reflection and by using the ladder of inference in three ways:

* Becoming more aware of your own thinking and reasoning (reflection);
* Making your thinking and reasoning more visible to others (advocacy);
* Inquiring into others' thinking and reasoning (inquiry).

Summation: When we just take notice and question ourselves about our assumptions, space is created for the possibility that our belief may not be the only way of seeing something. At the very least, we'll have fewer disagreements and a little less stress.

Management

FLUID MANAGEMENT STYLE OF A MULTI-GENERATIONAL LEADER…	
SILENT GENERATION NEEDS AN:	ADMINISTRATOR
BABY BOOMERS LOOK FOR A:	COACH
GENERATION X WANTS A:	FACILITATOR
GENERATION Y THRIVES UNDER A:	MENTOR

TABLE 4 MANAGEMENT STYLE OF A MULTI-GENERATIONAL LEADER

The management style of a multi-generational leader cannot and should not be fixed. It should be fluid, transparent and smart. From administrative to mentoring to coaching to facilitation – your management style must be ever-transforming.

As an administrator, the leader must create the direction of operations, set goals for production and manage the human resources of the department. This role is integral to all of the generations – as they all look for responsible direction. Though all generations require strong administration for daily operations, the Silent Generation in particular relies on formal direction for management.

As a mentor, the leader must set up opportunities for knowledge sharing. It can be suggested that one of the greatest compliments to a leader is the demonstration of knowledge that they have shared and has been put to work by their employees.

Mentorship is valuable to an organization because it is convenient and economic. It allows an organization to mold younger workers to their operating policies and objectives. E-mail mentoring is a top-notch way to start and maintain a "listen/advise" relationship between colleagues. It is practical, instant and non-geographical.

Mentorship through knowledge transfer also offers the prospect of setting up succession plans for the organization. Succession planning grooms younger generations to grow up the ranks of the organization through the guidance of mature generations. It ensures the progression of operations for future. Knowledge transfer is a valuable asset to organizations as well as a personal incentive to individuals.

As a coach, the leader must motivate the team. The coach supports weaknesses by providing training and resources for greater development.

As a facilitator, you must organize and coordinate the work of the group In doing this, you must retain the team's focus on the objective whilst maintaining communication and positively encouraging production.

Leading a successful project team requires that you develop strategies that maximize the strengths of each generation while managing the differences. This can include the types of tasks on which different team members work. This may mean actively allowing team members to self-select some of the tasks they wish to complete. Some choices may be aligned to generational preferences. For example, Silent Generation Sam may selected tasks that have longer timelines with greater project profile status, while Generation Y Yasmin wants to work on tasks where there would be immediate results.

Summation: Regardless of age, all employees seek a positive and collaborative relationship with their managers. Yet the grace period that Gen X or Gen Y employees will give you to get the relationship right is much shorter than that of Baby Boomers or the Silent Generation. The fact is that many leaders exhibit the management style that they experienced, often a top-down command and control approach. In most cases, this approach doesn't create the level of collaboration that is necessary for creating productive high-performance teams.

GENERATIONS – ASSETS			
The Silent Generation	**Baby Boomers**	**Generation X**	**Generation Y**
Loyal	Driven	Adaptable	Loyal
Reliable	Optimistic	Survivalist	Confident
Hardworking	Achievement oriented	Informal	Achievement oriented
Plays by the rules	Involved	Diversity	Inclusive
Service Oriented	Service oriented	Techno literacy	Techno literacy
Pleasant	Reads people	Entrepreneurial	Determined
Formal	Brainstorming	Thinks globally	Thinks globally
Detail-oriented	Multitasked	Creative	Multitasked
Traditional	Non-traditional	Non-traditional	Detail-oriented
Team oriented	Independent	Independent	Team oriented
Disciplined	Wants to please	Thinks outside the box	Thinks outside the box
Pioneers	Leaders	Innovators	Dedicated
Hands-on experience	Thinkers	Self-reliant	Diverse

TABLE 5 GENERATIONS - ASSETS

GENERATIONS – LIABILITIES			
The Silent Generation	**Baby Boomers**	**Generation X**	**Generation Y**
Hard to change	Judgmental	Cynical	Dependence
Strict	Sensitive to feedback	Sensitive to feedback	Expectation
Inexperience (technical)	Self-centered	Guarded	Inexperience (hands-on)
Hierarchal	Over confident	Careful	Over Confident
Boundary oriented	Impatient	Distrustful	Uncomfortable with conflict
Overly patient	Uncomfortable with conflict	Impatient	Needs structure
Micromanagement (prefers)	Inexperience (technical)	Micromanagement (dislikes)	Self-centred

TABLE 6 GENERATIONS - LIABILITIES

Communication

Communication is such an everyday, necessary tool it is often overlooked. With the invention of e-mail; the work world became smaller whilst the generation divide grew larger. Now, this isn't to say that e-mail is not a great communication tool. It certainly is. However, the generations have become so reliant on electronic mail that they are no longer speaking.

In the modern office, workers are more apt to send an e-mail to a co-worker than to walk over to their cubical (only steps away). This is difficult to accept by the

> Non-verbal communication or face and body language constitutes 93% of message

mature generations. It can be viewed as frivolous or lazy. *Why not just walk over and tell me in person?!* The Silent Generation and, to some extent, Baby Boomers relish in face to face meetings. It builds relationships. It allows a chance for discussion. Whether it is a quick update in the hall or a chat in the cubical – the mature generations are attracted to in-person interaction.

However, the younger generations find e-mail more effective and more efficient. Type. Click. Send. Done! Move on to the next task. With e-mail, Generation X multi-taskers can send a communication while they simultaneously have three other documents open on their taskbar at the same time. For Generation Y, the "on-demand generation", e-mail is convenient and mobile.

What about instant messaging? Mature generations find it bothering and annoying to have pop up notifications of instant messages (IM) and/or short messaging service (SMS). Mature generations want to *go to communications*. Like: going to the post office. Like: going to open a letter. *Go to communications* allows the Silent Generation and Baby Boomers to communicate and read communications on their time schedule. (It could be suggested that go to communications are a form of *pushed information*)

Younger generations want *pull to communication* (like *pulled information*). As such, e-mail, IM, DM and SMS are perfect tools for Generation X and Generation Y. Text me. Ping me. *Pulled to communications* allows Generation X and Generation Y to be pulled to communication wherever they are – whatever they might be doing.

A leader should consider what format the organization is using in communication with the generations. If the organization is using an instant messaging type of format, a team leader might understand the root of discontent with mature employees. It can cause frustration. Divide. Alternatively, if a Generation X or Generation Y employee is continually hit with stacks of paper-based memorandum, they may feel discontented. Frustration. Divide. What is a multi-generational leader to do about communication amongst the generations?

The best way to bridge the generation gap in terms of communication is to offer an array of formats. Not only is this a good way to calm *go to/pull to communications* frustrations it can also reduce generational stress and deescalate potential conflicts.

> According to Pew Internet and American Life Project statistics reported in February 2009, 90% of Internet Users between the ages of 18 and 72 use email.
>
> Over 70% of email users that are employed admit that they check their personal email at work an average of three times a day.
>
> Email can be both a big productivity tool (70% of people report email has enhanced their productivity) and a big waste of time (over 90% of email is spam).

Remember, the sections on Stress and Technology? Modern electronic communication is relatively new. As such, not all generations in the current workplace have confidence and experience using mass communication tools. This can cause a generation divide as some individuals can be left out of the loop. Being left out not only increases a divide but it fosters resentment which can potential become a conflict situation.

By offering an array of formats, an organization ensures that all stakeholders receive information in a timely manner. It also reinforces the message when the reader views it in multiple formats.

Introduce new digital communication tools slowly to allow for the team to adapt to the change. Ensure sufficient training on the tool along with a help desk, mentorship programme or tool squad for trouble-shooting and reference.

What are the preferred communications amongst the generations?

- The Silent Generation prefers paper-in-hand. They are linear and factual. They want to be able to jot notes down in margins and underline important information. The Silent Generation reads the daily newspaper, training materials and industry news from cover to cover. They want tangible paper-based-documents to refer back to later.
- Baby Boomers want structured paper-based-documents. They are organized yet creative. They want to be able to use a rainbow of coloured highlighters for important information. They read newspapers, self-help books and surf the internet. They like web-based information for reference.
- Generation X wants concise information fast. They are attracted to headlines, subheadings, news tickers, text boxes and tables. Whether the communication is paper-based or on-line, Generation X will be scanning for keywords.
- Generation Y marry the "communication wants" of the Silent Generation and Generation X. Like the Silent Generation, Generation Y are life-long readers. Like Generation X, Generation Y wants communication that attracts them visually.

When it comes to communication and interaction the generations vary. The Silent Generation can excel in both group work and unsupervised, independent, work. The Silent Generation experienced the team effort camaraderie of the war effort. They also experienced the drudgery of getting-things-done-because-they-had-to be-done during the depression days. With the marriage of team work and imposed independent chores the Silent Generation can work well in a team as well as alone.

Baby Boomers excel when communication and working in a group-like atmosphere. They enjoy interaction and discussion. However, they dislike role playing and other games sometimes used to open up communication channels.

Generation X gravitates to communication on an as-needed basis. They don't want to have a meeting just for the sake of having a meeting. They want communication to have a purpose. They prefer self-directed projects with little micro-management.

Generation Y is a team communicator all the way. They search for connections, communications and mentorship which provide personal challenge and teamwork. They are motivated to contribute and share with a team. Their teamwork doesn't end at 5pm – they will check in and chat up with their team after hours and on weekends.

It is advisable to create a communications go-to sheet for all four working generations, for example, a directory of "whom to call" for questions. Mature generations will appreciate the formality of a designated go-to person. Younger generations aren't shy to ask for help. Providing an in-house service desk in your organization can reduce exclusion based on lack of knowledge. It can also help bridge the generation gap by having your multi-generational team communicate (i.e. Silent Generation Sam connects with Generation X Xavier who is the go-to person for database questions.)

......

Incentives, Engagement and Retention

Incentives are powerful encouragement for individuals. A stimulating component to a role also helps retain valuable workers. They may feel more engaged. Valued. Appreciated. Energized. Recognized.

Let us first consider ways in which to offer stimulus to your workforce.

When one first thinks of employee incentives - it is automatic to envision bonus, salary raise, company car and/or paid vacation. Monetary incentives are nice things, yet harder and harder to come by in light of today's troubled economic times. It is valuable for organizations and leadership to consider non-monetary incentives which motivate the four working generations.

As previously noted in this book, mentorship is valuable incentive to an organization however it is also very important to individuals. Many members of the younger generations are attracted to mentorship programs for guidance throughout their professional development. For example, due to their own experience with their too-busy parents, (who often left them to their own devices) Generation X is attracted to positive guidance.

Mentors open up a form education that is inaccessible through book learning. Mentorship shares experiences, advises solutions and supports endeavors. Peer-to-peer mentorship grows interaction and bonds teammates.

Mentorship is also an immense communication tool to bridge the generations. Through mentorship programs, the four generations have a common ground on which to ask, discuss and brainstorm the challenges and solutions which arise in projects. It helps newcomers to a team navigate the operating system of an organization while allowing leading employees to impart their experience. The Silent Generation and Baby Boomers have the benefit of experience. Generation X and Generation Y have the asset of innovation. Mentorship is a forum in which the generations can bring to the table their "skill sets" to come up with solutions.

CORPORATE LADDER VS. CORPORATE LATTICE	
Corporate Ladder: The hierarchal order of rank in a corporation moving up and down.	Corporate Lattice: A twilled order of rank in a corporation moving up, down, diagonal and lateral.
• Fixed • Traditional • Steady • Adjusts to organization's needs	• Fluid • Modern • Can move faster or slower • Adjusts to individual's needs

TABLE 7 CORPORATE LADDER VS. CORPORATE LATTICE

Creating the framework for a corporate lattice can also be a valuable incentive to the four working generations. In a traditional corporate ladder, the employees must rise and descend the rungs of the corporate ladder depending on availability of jobs and the requirement of the organization. Movement up the corporate ladder can be stalled and slow. In a corporate lattice framework, workers can move up, down and laterally in job positions. The increase in career directionality opens up new opportunity and quicker motion for employees. More and more, the corporate lattice framework is being adopted by organizations as an incentive to employees as well as a measure of employee retention.

The fluid movement of a corporate lattice can be an incentive to many generations. It allows for employees to quicken or slow down their career motion depending on their balance of work/ life responsibilities. For mature generations, a lattice framework allows them to slowly descend the ladder. This is a perfect solution to members of the Silent Generation who choose to reduce working hours yet remain in the workforce. They can shift to less demanding roles within the organization with ease and dignity. This helps to push retirement further down the road while maintaining a salary for retirement planning for the more mature generations.

With the responsibilities of planning for retirement, pursuing personal interests and caring for dependents – Baby Boomers can use a corporate lattice to level their work/life duties.

This point is also shared by Generation X parents who take a parental leave. Returning to the workforce in the same capacity as pre-parenthood can be difficult due to child care hours, sick days, medical appointments and more. A corporate lattice allows the choice for a lateral move or downward shift of responsibilities to compensate for changing responsibilities at home. Plus in the corporate lattice, the generations have the ability to move upwards, laterally and in diagonal movements, in the future, when their responsibilities change.

A framework which makes allowance for the personal lives and career choices of the generations is also an employee retention strategy. It keeps valuable workers and retains their knowledge and expertise in the organization.

For Generation Y, a corporate lattice allows for a faster (faster in comparison to a corporate ladder framework) progression in an organization. There is more opportunity for movement, change of rank and additional accountability. It also presents opportunities for lateral moves to gain knowledge in other departments of the business - growing the Generation Y-er's general knowledge of the company and industry.

......

Another way to bridge the new generation gap and to provide incentive to a multi-generational team is to provide a meaningful corporate culture. Corporate culture is the philosophy, traditions and values which are unique to your organization. An organization can have greater worker retention when the organization's corporate culture is more attractive than that, of say, a competitor.

Now, this doesn't mean that need to turn your organization into a summer camp to make it have an attractive corporate culture. The business place is still a place of business. However, by giving meaning to your corporate culture you can create a connection between the generations and the entity. You can create solidarity for a common goal or purpose.

Providing a percentage of office-hours to pursue personal interests demonstrates a supportive corporate culture. It is also a great incentive. It can rejuvenate tired workers, get the creative juices flowing and reduce stress. However, office-hour incentive time is not a vacation and team members should appreciate the time as a perk (sorry folks, no paid days off here!).

Incentives for Professional Development

- Consider inviting a speaker to present wealth management strategies and income tax regulations for help with retirement planning for members of the Silent Generation.
- Think about arranging for the Human Resources department to compile file on community organizations and services for the elderly - to help Baby Boomers manage the care of their aging parents.
- Consider supporting Generation X and Y to use a percentage of company time for on-line coursework or webinars in line with their function in the organization.
- Offer mentoring in your organization.

Other incentives can be multi-generational and inclusive. They can contribute to the bonding of the generations as well as overall well being.

Work/life balance incentives

- Group yoga class at lunch.
- Coordinating a 5K running clinic.
- Subsidize gym or fitness memberships.
- Common area with television for major events, such as the World Cup Finals and Olympics.
- Offer an ongoing seminar series on all the issues that will be important to your staff – nutrition, elder care, parenting, time management, financial management.

Work environment incentives

- Evaluate flexible positions and job autonomy to allow more work-life balance in terms of schedule control.
- Enable individuals to work-without-wires by providing laptops.
- Set up group work stations (tables and chairs or a couch and long table)
- Set up Wi-Fi (so that people can use their laptops at the group work station)
- In-house convenience centres allow workers to spend less time running around making them more productive workers and less stressed individuals. These services include:
  o Bank machine
  o Dry cleaning
  o On-site daycare
  o Ticket buying/concierge service
- Give your physical office space character (art work, murals, inspirational signage)
- Allow individuals to customize their cubicles (family pictures, post cards)
- Provide healthy lunch options, reasonably priced, in the organization's cafeteria. (An upgrade from this is to provide healthy lunch options, locally grown or produced, in the organization's cafeteria. Fast food, college cuisine and foods-from-a-box are generally high-fat, high-calorie foods. Locally grown fruits and vegetables are a smart alternative. It will contribute to better nutrition, digestion and over-all energy of team members. It will also demonstrate the organization's commitment to community responsibility; contributing to the local economy, supporting local farmers and reducing carbon emission created by food transportation)

Along the lines of community responsibility…an organization can bridge the new generation gap by providing a platform of shared causes. Take the above example of healthy food choices in the cafeteria. Baby Boomers are concerned with high cholesterol. Generation X is concerned with global warming. Locally grown food choices in the cafeteria is a solution to the concerns of these two groups (lower cholesterol because of more nutritious foods and a hit against global warming because of less carbon emissions). Corporate social responsibility can also happen very locally within the organization, such as recycling initiatives, healthy food outreach, and energy saving tips.

Environmentally responsible incentives

- Encourage ride sharing to off-site meetings.
- Enable teleconferencing
- Provide a shuttle service from trains to office for commuting workers
- Provide well-lit, secure, bike posts to encourage peddle powered commutes to the office.
- Provide a battery of bikes for off-site, local, meetings (paint them in your organization's colours or put your logo on it for advertising)

Additionally, an organization can bridge the new generation gap by participating in community events which bring the generations together. This is a real-world example of diversity in action.

Perhaps your team participates in a walk for cancer. Everyone, of every generation, has been touched by cancer in one way or another. It is a global cause which hits home. It invokes action, passion and commitment from the four generations. From Silent Generation Sam to Generation Y Yasmin – the team walks together, spends time together, motivates each other and succeeds together. The organization donates time and money to an important charity (for which they receive recognition and a charitable tax receipt). The organization also, by walking together, encourages an activity that has team building results - a win-win result for everyone involved.

Music in the workplace is the one incentive which divides the generations. Generation X and Generation Y appreciate being able to tune in to their portable music devices at the workplace. However, the Silent Generation and Baby Boomers often take the younger generation's "tuning in" as "tuning out" (i.e. detaching themselves from the workplace). So does music in the office build invisible walls contributing to the new generation gap?

It depends. To some teams music can be motivational and bonding. Who doesn't like a little Ella Fitzgerald in the background?!...Well, perhaps Generation X Xavier prefers Green Day whereas Generation Y Yasmin prefers Common. If the generations don't agree on musical choice it can cause teeth-gritting-resentment and conflict.

A solution would be to rotate music in which case each generation is exposed to the other's musical preferences. Or, you could choose to have a no-music-in-the-office policy to ensure no one is tuning in/out on company time. [Note: Just remember to send an e-mail as well as a paper-based memorandum to ensure all generations get the message!]

......

Motivating elements in an organization can help retain valuable workers in an organization. In light of aging demographics, changing home life responsibilities, and the labour market, it is smart for organizations to devise strategies to retain their talent. However, incentives are only one element in employee retention.

One of the most important strategies in retaining workers is to engage them. Engagement is when an employee acts in ways in which they seek more involvement in their roles to further the organizational mandate. Basically, it is the concept of making an individual feel valued in the organization. This is tied to that individual's productivity and organizational loyalty. If an employee feels engaged in the workplace they are much more likely to remain with that organization.

> Highly committed employees perform up to 20 percentile points better than less committed employees, and are 87% less likely to leave the organization than employees with low levels of commitment.

SILENT GENERATION:	• Make time for personal interactions • Demonstrate respect for history and tradition • Embrace hallmarks of family values and good manners • Be linear and logical emphasizing relevant facts • Create opportunities to socialize, particularly between assignments • Honour hard work with formal recognition
BABY BOOMERS	• Ask for their input and expertise. • Allow them avenues to build consensus • Give them public recognition and awards for their work • Provide them perks in line with their professional status • Place them in charge of projects that build name recognition and demonstrate their leadership savvy
GENERATION X	• Allow them to prioritize projects as they see fit • Offer regular feedback (constructive and critical) • Encourage the pursuit of interests outside of work • Create opportunities for fun at work • Utilize the latest computer technology • Provide perks as requested
GENERATION Y	• Demonstrate leadership and coaching skills • Create opportunities that encourage working with friends • Recognize and support personal goals • Respect their personal achievements and emerging professional credibility • Build working relationships that are collaborative in nature • Be flexible about their work schedules and assignments

TABLE 8: IDEAS FOR EMPOWERING THE GENERATIONS AT WORK

Engagement is very necessary to an organization's ability to survive and even grow. Engagement places value on the generations; making them more productive workers. The environment of a work place can bridge the new generation gap by being a healthy, happy, supportive environment. However, in the case where there is engagement breakdown and an employee has a failed to perform, an effective leader must have a Plan B.

For underperforming workers, a Personal Improvement Plans (PIP) is sometimes required. A PIP is informal contract between a supervisor and employee which clearly communicates improvement points and set dates for achieving them. It is a sort of wake-up-call to an employee notifying them that their performance is not up to the standard of their role. [Note: Failure to meet the PIP improvement points or deadline dates usually results in disciplinary action or even termination. However, in some cases, PIPs can offer a real plan for improvement to disengaged workers.]

PIPs work well with the Silent Generation and Generation Y who are accustomed to a coaching situation. They value feedback, guidance on what to improve and schooling on how to make the improvements. These two generations, want to please authority and as such PIPs can be effective tools to steer them in the corrected direction.

However, tread lightly when using PIPs with Baby Boomers and Generation X, as both generations sometimes take the term "improvement" to mean "critique". These generations take less-than-positive feedback as judgments or even personal attacks.

It is advisable, to hold an annually, or bi-annually, confidential, one-on-one performance review with all members of your team. It allows a formal occasion whereby members of the Silent Generation can discuss challenges and solutions. The Silent Generation will not, casually pop their heads in their leader's office for a quick chat about something. It goes against their nature. However, a scheduled meeting for the purpose of review is a prime opportunity for them to bring out their hand-written notes about their concerns.

A one-on-one performance review provides Baby Boomers the chance to connect on a personal level with their team leaders. It is a chance to rant and rave. Baby Boomers know their clients and third-party stakeholders better than head office. They should be provided an opportunity to share concerns, challenges and success stories with their team leader.

A one-on-one review provides Generation X and Generation Y with guidance on their professional development, recognizes their strengths and addresses challenges. These are the generations that have grown up with significant feedback throughout their schooling, as well as the often undivided attention of their parents. Performance reviews, rather than an issue that causes stress, should be seen as a forum for all parties involved to discuss positive acknowledgements and attributes as well as identify areas for growth.

Personal Improvement Plans and reviews are means of employee engagement. In both circumstances, reviewers should focus on the positive contributions and strengths of all employees, and use the opportunity of a review to help employees feel valued.

A Compliment Cookie is when you provide feedback in layers.

First layer: positive feedback
Second layer: constructive feedback on what could/needs-to be improved
Third layer: positive feedback

. . . . . .

Mature Worker Retention

There are many on-line and in-print destinations available to help a worker get out of his/her current job situation (résumé services, industry database, magazine features, job boards, career advice). However, there are limited resources for individuals who want to stay or return to the workforce in a more customized capacity.

Consider this question: Does your organization take steps to recruit older workers (past traditional retirement age)? Many members of the Silent Generation and Baby Boomers have interest in working past their official retirement age. As previously discussed in this book, some aging workers are financially unprepared to retire. Others still love their work and want to continue contributing to their workplace. This is a prime opportunity for organizations to tap into the mature workers' knowledge and experience.

Taking on a mature worker as a special projects consultant or ongoing employee can be of great benefit to the organization. Mature workers can fill job gaps in labour shortages. They can ease upper management transitions. They are adept at taking on responsibility and leadership. They are a willing workforce which, due to their experience, requires little micro-management.

......

Younger Worker Retention

To retain younger workers, organizations must present opportunity for development. Not only up the corporate lattice, but also through personal and professional growth. Offering challenging work is one way to retaining Generation X and Y. Another, is to offer work with a greater meaning. Generation X wants to have a purpose and Generation Y wants to save the world. By tapping into these ambitions, an organization can present attractive reasons to resist job movement.

Generation X and Y also want to see the money. This generation has higher post-secondary debt than the previous generations, more expensive housing options, and live in a much more materially oriented society. Bonuses and competitive salaries are an important factor to consider when wanting to retain superstar employees.

......

Dos and Don'ts of retaining the generations

DO encourage the Silent Generation to share their experience. Respect is a core value to the Silent Generation.

DO NOT treat the Silent Generation as another old fogey. They have stayed in their workplace because their contributions are valued by many.

DO encourage Baby Boomers to be part of the decision-making process. Inclusiveness is a core value to Baby Boomers.

DO NOT focus on failures with Baby Boomers. They are goal oriented, and experienced enough to learn from failures and succeed the next time.

DO encourage increased responsibility and creativity with Generation X. Independence is a core value with Generation X.

DO NOT micromanage Generation X. They are capable, and self-directed.

DO train Generation Y on how do to a job. Education is a core value of Generation Y.

DO NOT assume with Generation Y. Presumptions based on age or experience of the youngest generation often means we miss out on their most useful skills and attributes.

......

Summation: Across the board, every generation wants to be recognized, engaged and respected in their organization. The generation gap occurs when an individual becomes disenchanted with the organization, their role or their team. Incentives, employee engagement and retention efforts should be aimed at contributing to a better quality of life for the generations (both inside and outside the office environment).

......

The nature of the new generation gap occurs through exclusion and misunderstanding. Inclusion bridges the divide; creating a foundation on which a responsive leader can build, with the four working generations, organizational accomplishment. Information flows in all directions in effective learning-driven, collaborative, creative organizations. The most successful leaders find a way to let every generation be heard. They recognize that no one has all the answers, yet, together, everyone can contribute to the solutions.

....

Chapter 5

Fact or Fiction?

1. FACT OR FICTION? The Silent Generation is "out of touch".
    FICTION. While the Silont Generation may be inexperienced with some newer digital technologies they are very much in-the-know about current markets. The Silent Generation reads newspapers daily, industry reports, political trends and global events. They are a very informed generation.

    A strength of the Silent Generation is their knowledge of customers and stakeholders. The Silent Generation entered into the workforce when customer service and handshakes were top priority. They make connecting with external stakeholders a priority. They know clients by name and by face.

2. FACT OR FICTION? Baby Boomers are a sandwich generation.
    FACT. Baby Boomers are sandwiched between caring for their aging Silent Generation parents and their evolving Generation Y children. Due to this, Baby Boomers can be stretched emotionally, financially and physically between their dependents and work.

3. FACT OR FICTION? Generation X is overly casual. FACT. It is true Generation X is more informal than previous generations. One could call them casual. They come to the office in jeans, don't want to be referred to with courtesy titles (Mr. & Mrs. So-and-so – that's their high school teachers!). They will knock-off at 4pm on a Friday to get a head start on the weekend. Being casual should not be confused with being lazy. Generation X is a highly project dedicated group. They are able to effectively multi-task, prioritize and innovate according to latest trends. Generation X can get more done, in less time, than other generations.

4. FACT OR FICTION? Generation Y expect to be CEO – now. FICTION. Though Generation Y is accustomed to instant stardom (every child gets a participant trophy!) they do understand they must move up the corporate lattice like everyone else. Generation Y looks for opportunities to contribute meaningfully to projects. They appreciate mentorship to guide them in their careers.

. . . .

Who's Who of the Generations

WHO'S WHO OF THE GENERATIONS	
The Silent Generation	• Gloria Steinem (Activist) • Harry Belafonte (Singer) • Margaret Atwood (Writer) • Barbra Streisand (Singer) • Phil Donahue (Talk-show host) • Neil Armstrong (Astronaut) • Woody Allen (Director) • Paul Simon (Musician) • Clint Eastwood (Actor/Director)
Baby Boomers	• Oprah Winfrey (Media personality) • Bill Gates (Microsoft Founder) • Karin Kain (Ballerina) • Ozzy Osborne (Singer) • Steven Spielberg (Director) • Sting (Singer) • John Travolta (Actor) • Stephen King (Author) • Joan Jett (Singer)
Generation X	• Michael Dell (Dell Computing Founder) • Jeff Bezos (Founder of Amazon) • Will Smith (Actor) • Eddie Murphy (Comedian/Actor) • Wayne Gretzky (NHL player) • The Edge (Rock guitarist) • Chuck Palahniuk (Author) • Garry Kasparov (Chess champion)
Generation Y	• Beyoncé (Singer) • Justin Bieber (Singer) • Selena Gomez (Singer/Actor) • Zac Efron (Actor) • Michael Phelps (Olympian) • LeBron James (NBA Athlete) • Mark Zuckerberg (Facebook Founder)

TABLE 9 WHO'S WHO OF THE GENERATIONS

Top 10 Skills of a Multi-Generational Leader

TOP 10 SKILLS OF A MULTI-GENERATIONAL LEADER		
Foster	☑	Coaching
Focus	☑	Listening
Respect	☑	Innovation
Understanding	☑	Trust
Communication	☑	Mentor

TABLE 10 SKILLS OF A MULTI-GENERATIONAL LEADER

......

Quick Reference of Technology Terms

RSS Feed: RSS stands for Really Simple Syndication. It is used to publish frequently updated works like blogs and news headlines.

Example: Headline News.

Blog: A web log. An on-line space to write journal-like entries.

Think: http://michelledagninosblog.blogspot.com/

Vlog: A video blog or site which uses video content.

Example: YouTube

Podcast: a web based audio broadcast via an RSS feed to subscribers.

Example: CBC radio podcasts.

Webinar: a web based seminar to exchange information.

Example: nielson-online.com

Wiki: A collaborative website where content can be uploaded/updated/ edited by anyone who has access to it.

Example: wikipedia

SMS: SMS stands for Short Messaging System. With a mobile phone one can send a short message (using 160 alphanumeric characters) to other mobile phones.

Example: Text messages.

DM: Direct message

Example: Twitter

PING ME: tech term for "call me" or "remind me"

Example: Text messages

GPS: GPS stands for Global Positioning System. It uses a series of satellites, computers and receivers to determine the latitude and longitude of a receiver.

Example: Google maps

Smart Device: a machine which is designed to perform user-friendly functions like e-mailing, calling, word pressing, calculating, scheduling, etc…

Example: Personal Digital Assistants (PDAs), Blackberry, iPhone

---

Here are some most commonly used text message short forms:

2moro – Tomorrow
2nite – Tonight
ASAP – As Soon As Possible
B4N – Bye For Now
BCNU – Be Seeing You
BRB – Be Right Back
BTW – By The Way
CWYL – Chat With You Later
CYA – See Ya
DK – Don't Know
F2F – Face To Face
FWIW – For What It's Worth
GR8 – Great
IMAO – In My Arrogant Opinion
IMHO – In My Humble Opinion
IRL – In Real Life
ISO – In Search Of
JK – Just Kidding
K – Okay
L8R – Later
LMAO – Laughing My Arse Off
LMK – Let Me Know
LOL – Laughing Out Loud
NIMBY – Not In My Back Yard
NP – No Problem

OMG – Oh My God
OT – Off Topic
PPL – People
POV – Point Of View
RBTL – Read Between The Lines
ROTFLMAO – Rolling On The
    Floor Laughing My Arse Off
RT – Real Time
THX , TX and THKS – Thanks
SITD – Still In The Dark
SYS – See You Soon
RTM – Read The Manual
TLC – Tender Loving Care
TMI – Too Much Information
TTYL – Talk To You Later
TYVM – Thank You Very Much
UOK – Are You Okay?
WRUD – What Are You Doing?
WYWH – Wish You Were Here

Employee Engagement Survey

ORGANIZATION | MULTI-GENERATIONAL DIVERSITY SURVEY

Dear team member:
At our organization, we value your feedback. Please fill out the following survey and return it to the departmental suggestion box by the end of the week.   Your feedback is completely anonymous. We appreciate your participation!

Date:	
Team Leader:	
Department:	

Area of Interest	Strongly Agree	Agree	Disagree	Strongly Disagree	Don't Know
Our organization is inclusive to all generations of workers					
Our organization supports multi-generational inclusion through:					
Diversity training					
Workshops on working with a multi-generational team					
Workshops on leading a multi-generational team					
Multi-generational teams					
Multi-generational team building activities					
Materials for multi-generational inclusion					
Other (please specify):					
Multi-generational inclusion is not supported					
I feel my generation is respected by management.					
I feel my generation is respected by others in the organization.					
I enjoy working with other generations on projects.					
I learn from working with other generations on projects.					
The organization should offer more opportunities to work with other generations on projects.					

Area of Interest	Strongly Agree	Agree	Disagree	Strongly Disagree	Don't Know
I have experienced discrimination, in this organization, because of my generation/age.					
I feel my colleagues have experienced discrimination, in this organization, because of their generation/age.					
There is bias, in this organization, based on generation/age.					
Management addresses discrimination, based on generation/age in this organization.					
I feel welcomed in this organization.					
The views of various generations are seriously considered when making decisions in this organization.					
Workers have a good understanding of generational policies in this organization.					
COMMENTS					
Please expand upon your assessment of any areas in which our organization could improve their multi-generational support. We welcome your suggestions!					

TABLE 11 EMPLOYEE ENGAGEMENT SURVEY

BIBLIOGRAPHY

"12 Questions to Measure Employee Engagement". <u>Workforce Management Online.</u> October 2003.

Armour, Stephanie. "Generation Y: They've arrived at work with a new attitude". <u>USA Today</u>. 6 Nov. 2005.

Argyris, Chris. <u>Overcoming Organizational Defenses: Facilitating Organizational Learning.</u> New York: Prentice Hall, 1990.

Begley, Sharon and Interlandi, Jeneen. "The Dumbest Generation? Don't be Dumb" <u>Newsweek</u>. 2, Jun. 2008.

"Blog" Random House Dictionary. <u>Random House</u>, Inc. 2009.

Bonesveld, Sarah. "Whippersnappers in the workplace" <u>Globe and Mail</u>. 12 Jan. 2009.

Brusilow, Rafael. "Job autonomy blurs work-life balance: Study" Metro Canada. 13 Jan. 2009.

Burgman, Tamsyn. "Vulnerable Gen-Y-ers seeking ways to cope" Amhurst Daily News, <u>CP Press</u>, 26 Feb. 2009.

"Corporate Ladder" Random House Dictionary, Random House, Inc. 2009.

Deal, Jennifer. J. <u>Retiring the Generation Gap – How Employees Young & Old Can Find Common Ground</u>. New York, John Wiley & Sons, 2007.

De Kort, Lana. "White Paper: Generations at Work" <u>AFAIM</u>, 2004.

"Different generations want different things from work" <u>Waterloo Region Record</u>. 30 Aug. 2008.

Encyclopedia Britinica Online; <u>Encyclopaedia Britannica Online Library Edition</u>. 26 Mar. 2009.

"Generation Y: The Millennials – Ready or not, here they come<u>" NAS Recruitment Communications.</u> 2006.

"Global Positioning Service" <u>The American Heritage Dictionary of the English Language,</u> Fourth Edition, 2009.

"General Social Survey: Paid and unpaid work", The Daily, <u>Statistics Canada</u>. 19 Jul. 2006.

Howe, Denis. "Short Message Service" <u>The Free On-line Dictionary of Computing</u>, 2007.

"Lady Windermere's Fan, III". <u>Bartlett's Familiar Quotations</u>. London. 2002.

Langton, Jerry. "Boomers feeling financial squeeze" <u>The Toronto Star</u>. 21 Jan. 2009.

Langton, Jerry. "Can Boomers rely on public purse?" <u>The Toronto Star</u>. 21 Jan. 2009.

"Managing the Facebookers" Business. <u>The Economist</u>. 3 Jan. 2009.

Marshall, Katherine and Ferrao, Vincent. "Perspectives on Labour and Income – August 2007" <u>Statistics Canada.</u> 21 Nov. 2008.

Menon, Vinjay. "Back off, Google, you're too close" <u>The Toronto Star</u>. 5 Feb. 2009.

Milic, Corina. "At 25, I'm looking for a second career" <u>The Toronto Star</u>. 31, Jan. 2009.

Nebenzahl, Donna. "Engaged workers expect more but they produce more, too" The Gazette. 7 Apr. 2007

Parr, James. "Tips for Baby Boomers keen to stay employed" Financial Post. 30 May 2007.

Pontell, Jonathan. "Stuck in the Middle" USA Today. 27 May 2009.

Rose, Fine-Meyer, Gibson, Stephanie. Advertising: Reflections of Culture and Values. Rubison Education. 2002.

"RSS Feed" Webster's New Millennium Dictionary of English. 2009.

Salkowitz, Rob. Generation Blend – Managing Across the Technology Age Gap.
New York: John Wiley & Sons, 2008.

Sankey, Derek. "Keeping Older Workers" CanWest News Service. 27 Jan. 2009.

"Study: Returning to the Parental Home", The Daily, Statistics Canada. 3 Oct. 2006.

Tapscott, Don and Williams, Anthony. Wikinomics – How Mass Collaboration Changes Everything. New York. Penguin Group, 2006.

Tapscott, Don. Growing Up Digital. New York. McGraw-Hill. 2009.

Thau, Richard. And Heflin, Jay. ed. Generations Apart – Xers Vs. Boomers Vs. The Elderly. New York: Prometheus Books. 1997.

"Today in history" [Final Edition], Edmonton Journal. 26 May 2007.

Torisk, Emmalee, C. "Generation Y heavily dependent on technology, promotes laziness" The Jambar. Sept. 25, 2008.

"Vlog" <u>Random House Dictionary</u>. 2009

Mader, Stewart. <u>Wikipatterns</u>. New York: Wiley Publishing, 2008.

Senge, Peter. <u>The Fifth Discipline Fieldbook.</u> New York: Crown Business, 2006.

Williams, Cara. "The Sandwich Generation" <u>Statistics Canada</u>. 2005.

White, Nancy J. "30s are the new 20s for Gen Y". <u>The Toronto Star</u>. 20 Feb. 2009.

"Wiki" <u>The American Heritage Dictionary of the English Language</u>, Fourth Edition. 2009.

"Who Are the Generations?" <u>Bridgeworks</u>. 2007.

Zemke, Rob. Et al. <u>Generations at Work – Managing the Clash of Vetrans, Boomers, Xers and Nexters in Your Workplace</u>. Performance Research Associates. 2000.

......

INDEX

INDEX OF TABLES AND FIGURES

INDEX OF TABLES

INDEX OF FIGURES

ABOUT THE AUTHOR

 Michelle Dagnino is a social entrepreneur, lawyer, consultant and speaker. She is one of North America's leading experts on youth engagement and generational change.

Michelle's unique expertise makes her a sought-after public speakers on Gen y engagement, youth leadership, and managing the multi-generational workforce. As a global lecturer on these topics, she has made hundreds of presentations to tens of thousands of audience members in regards to connecting to young people, understanding how to motivate Millennials in the workplace, and how to meaningfully engage youth in society.

Michelle's innovative and thought-provoking work has garnered her over a dozen awards including the 2004 YWCA Young Woman of Distinction award. Her high profile work also lead to Maclean's calling her "one of the Top 25 Leaders under 30" in Canada. She has been the frequent subject of various newspaper and magazine articles, including cover stories in magazines across Canada, has been featured in dozens of other media; and has been the subject of two documentaries. The Toronto Star named her "a woman to buoy the soul", and the City of Toronto honoured her with the Person's Day Award in recognition of her leadership and contributions to the community. In November 2006 Michelle was named by The Globe and Mail and the Women's Executive Network as one of Canada's Top 100: Most Powerful Women.

Dagnino is a graduate of Osgoode Hall Law School and holds a Master's degree in Political Science.

What can Michelle Dagnino do for my organization?

Michelle provides organizations with policies and directives that motivate management and staff to be proactive leaders in their communities and workplaces. Examples of Michelle's work have been to develop training initiatives, incentive and recognition programs, corporate culture evaluations, mentorship programs and more.

With her keen understanding of the millennial generation, Michelle can help your company focus on how to recruit and retain this valuable young resource, ensuring the future success of your company and your employees.

......